DEMONOLOGY

101

Demons, Spiritual Warfare, and Self Deliverance Prayers

DANIEL C. OKPARA

Copyright © October 2020 by Daniel C. Okpara.

Published By:

Better Life Media.

BETTER LIFE WORLD OUTREACH CENTER.

Website: www.BetterLifeWorld.org

Email: info@betterlifeworld.org

FOLLOW US ON FACEBOOK

Like our Page on Facebook for updates:

https://facebook.com/betterlifeworld/

This title and others are available for quantity discounts for sale promotions, gifts, and evangelism. Visit our website or email us to get started.

Any scripture quotation in this book is taken from the King James Version or New International Version, except where stated—used by permission.

All texts, calls, letters, testimonies, and inquiries are welcome.

Are you looking for resources to keep your spirit on fire?

Follow me on my Facebook (PRIVATE GROUP) for daily 30-minute morning broadcast. Stir your spirit for Jesus every morning. Start and end your day with powerful prayers and teachings and command your breakthrough.

JOIN NOW FOR FREE

www.bit.ly/fb-danielokpara

CONTENTS

Receive Daily and Weekly Prayers

Powerful Prayers Sent to Your Inbox Every Monday

Enter your email address to receive notifications of new posts, prayers and prophetic declarations sent to you by email.

Email Address

Sign Me Up

*Go to: **BreakThroughPrayers** to subscribe to receive FREE WEEKLY PRAYER POINTS, and prophetic declarations sent to you by email.*

www.breakthroughprayers.org

FREE BOOKS

Download These 4 Powerful Books Today for FREE... Take Your Relationship With God to a New Level.

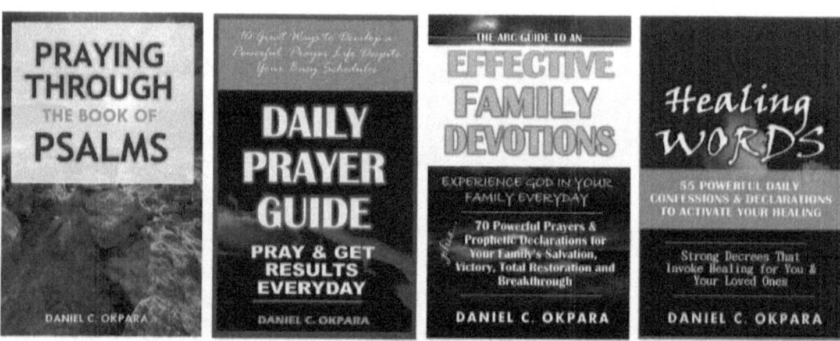

Click Here to Download

www.betterlifeworld.org/grow

INTRODUCTION

C.S Lewis, the famous nineteenth-century Christian Apologist, said:

"There are two equal and opposite errors into which our race can fall about the devils. One is to disbelieve in their existence. The other is to believe and to feel an excessive and unhealthy interest in them. They themselves are equally pleased by both errors ..."

It's been decades since he said that, the Church is still battling with these equal and opposite extremes. We have people who believe that demons and deliverance teachings and practices are a wish-wash emotional razzmatazz used to fleece people into an undue advantage. They believe that once we become Christians, old things are passed away. That demons have no more power over the believer's life.

Of course, that's right. But that's not the complete truth. The Bible tells us that we are in ongoing warfare. Demonic powers are not dead yet. They are still very much alive and contending with our lives and faith in various ways. To ignore their existence or assume they have no power is absolute ignorance; one that the devil himself is happy about.

On the other hand, some virtually live, talk and smell demons. It's all about demons and nothing else. They believe that all their problems in life are from demons. They spend hours binding and casting demons, running to and fro for one deliverance or the other; and as it were, they never seem to be delivered. These Christians make themselves prayer projects, believing that the reason they are where they are is because they are under some curse or that one witch out there is after them.

This is also the wrong way to approach the subject of demons. We need a balance between both extremes.

First, demons exist for real and have real powers to cause havoc and damage. They are not a fabrication of our imaginations. The Bible paints a picture of them as real, evil beings that create actual problems, hindrances, and crisis. They are not just ***what we think about*** and can wish out with just motivational, positive thoughts. Not at all. We need to learn how to recognize their operations, projections, and attacks and rebuke them, cast them out and obtain deliverance where necessary.

However, we are not, as believers, to become what I call demon hunters. That is, a kind of emotional lifestyle that escalates and celebrates the activities of demons more than that of God; one that spends more time discoursing demons than the power of God.

When we sense and recognize demonic operations, we must stand in the authority of God's Word and rebuke them, cast them out and obtain deliverance in Christ. But we must not assume that all problems that we face in life are demons. More so, we are not meant to be scared of demons, because, by position, God has placed us in a more place of power than them. God has given us the ability to overcome them.

In this Bible Study, I want to answer most questions about demons. These answers are designed for an everyday Christian, so I have avoided all the heavy sounding Greek and etymological vocabularies that mystify the subject, and focused mainly on the Bible truths. I am convinced that these answers and teachings will bless you. But more importantly, they will empower you to resist demonic operations in your life and family, and obtain deliverance and breakthrough.

"When we sense and recognize demonic operations, we must stand in the authority of God's Word and rebuke them, cast them out and obtain deliverance in Christ."

1

WHAT ARE DEMONS?

---

14 Thou art the anointed cherub that covereth; and I have set thee so: thou wast upon the holy mountain of God; thou hast walked up and down in the midst of the stones of fire.

15 Thou wast perfect in thy ways from the day that thou wast created, till iniquity was found in thee.

16 By the multitude of thy merchandise, they have filled the midst of thee with violence, and thou hast sinned: therefore I will cast thee as profane out of the mountain of God: and I will destroy thee, O covering cherub, from the midst of the stones of fire.

[17] Thine heart was lifted up because of thy beauty; thou hast corrupted thy wisdom because of thy brightness: I will cast thee to the ground, I will lay thee before kings, that they may behold thee. **- Ezekiel 28:14-17**

At the mention of demons, we often picture images drawn from primitive paintings. We picture frightening flying creatures with horns, fangs and claws, such as appear in movies, video games, and comic books, waging a battle against all that's good. Unfortunately, these images do not tell how demons actually look like and how they operate. The Bible is the best place to discover and learn about demons and their operations.

The scripture above talks about the anointed Cherub. Scholars agree that this personality is no other than Lucifer. He walked in majesty and glory until his heart began to be lifted because of his beauty. He became discontent of his position as Heaven's chief musician. He wanted to be like God.

> *For he said in his heart, "I will ascend to heaven and rule the angels. I will take the highest throne. I will preside on the Mount of Assembly far away in the north. I will climb to the highest heavens and be like the Most High"* - Isaiah 14:13-14
>
> - TLB.

Can you imagine that? He said...

- I will ascend to heaven and rule the angels

- I will take the highest throne

- I will preside over the assembly

- I will climb the highest heaven and be like the Most High

In his pride, arrogance, and corruption, he influenced one-third of angels. They carried out a rebellion in heaven. But they lost. The book of Revelation chapter 12 gives a picture of what happened after they lost.

7Then there was war in heaven; Michael and the angels under his command fought the dragon and his hosts of fallen angels. 8And the Dragon lost the battle and was forced from heaven.

9This great Dragon—the ancient serpent called the devil, or Satan, the one deceiving the whole world—was thrown down onto the earth with all his army.

₁₀Then I heard a loud voice shouting across the heavens, "It has happened at last! God's salvation and the power and the rule, and the authority of his Christ are finally here; for the Accuser of our brothers has been thrown down from heaven onto earth—he accused them day and night before our God.

₁₁ They defeated him by the blood of the Lamb and by their testimony; for they did not love their lives but laid them down for him.

*₁₂Rejoice, O heavens! You citizens of heaven, rejoice! Be glad! But woe to you people of the world, for the devil has come down to you in great anger, knowing that he has little time." – **Rev. 12:7-12***

Satan staged a coup in heaven. However, he lost, and thus was cast out. He and his angels now live in other heavenly places and carry out attacks against human beings on earth.

Accordingly, demons are former angels who followed Lucifer. They joined satan in a rebellion against God in heaven which they lost.

We don't know the exact time this holy war took place, but the Bible is clear that it did happen.

Right now, demons still follow the leadership of their principal, satan. Their goal remains to corrupt people's minds against God, His plan of salvation and oppose the people of God.

Just like angels, demons have emotions, will, intellect, power and own thoughts. Out of their own choices, they chose to become evil. So all their works are evil and conform to the will of the devil. Though they are spiritual beings, they can sometimes take on physical forms to accomplish their programs.

Just as God's angels praise God and help believers, satan and his demons slander God's name on earth and work towards the destruction and deception of all those who love and serve God.

> **Be careful—watch out for attacks from Satan, your great enemy. He prowls around like a hungry, roaring lion, looking for some victim to tear apart** - 1 Peter 5:8 TLB.

The greatest mission of satan and his demons are hindering the Gospel. 2 Corinthians 4:4 says, *"In whom the god of this world hath blinded the minds of them which believe not, lest the light of the glorious gospel of Christ, who is the image of God, should shine unto them."*

In many places, the Bible calls demons, "evil spirits," and "unclean spirits," and states that they attack Christians and do battle with the holy angels.

Though demons are powerful and can cause serious problems, the Bible says they have been defeated. Satan may be the prince of this world, but we are now reigning with the King. Greater is He who is in us than those who are in the world.

As children of God, we have the power to resist the devil and his demons and command their operations to cease in our lives and family.

"Demons are former angels who followed Lucifer. They joined satan in a rebellion against God in heaven which they lost."

2

ORIGIN OF DEMONS

---

*All things were made by him; and without him was not anything made that was made - **John 1:3***

*For by him were all things created, that are in heaven, and that are in earth, visible and invisible, whether they be thrones, or dominions, or principalities, or powers: all things were created by him and for him. - **Colossians 1:16.***

God created all things, visible and invisible; and that includes demons. That's how they came to be. But they were not created as demons.

They were created as angels, with a will and ability to make their own choices. They chose to join Lucifer in his rebellion against God. Thus, when they were defeated, they were chased out of heaven.

Demons are former angels who chose to rebel against God. They are beings who have lost all their glory

---

Some ancient traditions argue that demons are not fallen angels but the remains or spirits of the mutilated bodies of the vast evil humans who perished in flood. Others claim that demons are products of the corruption that took place in Genesis chapter six, where it is written that spirit beings (possibly angels) had sex with physical women. Unfortunately, these arguments disagree with the scriptures.

First, we know that unsaved dead are in Hades and not roaming the earth (Psalm 9:17; Luke 16:23; Revelation 20:13). Secondly, demons have been in existence even before the corruption that took place in Genesis chapter six.

God made all things, and that includes demons. So it's in order and Biblical to state that demons are angels lured into rebellion by satan. They are now satan's messengers. Together they go about stealing, killing and destroying.

God created all things, visible and invisible; and that includes demons. That's how they came to be.

3

DEMONS IN THE OLD TESTAMENT

There are many references to demons in the Old Testament. But they are not talked about as demons per se.

Why?

There are two possible reasons for that.

1. The Old Testament is focused on talking about God, His Sovereignty, and the Covenant. The writers wanted to teach the hearers about faithfulness to the Covenant between God and His people.

2. The second possible reason is that language itself had to evolve. The prophets spoke words that made sense to their original audience. That audience had no understanding of the Bible in its complete form. It was not until the *Inter-Testament* period that there was a terminology available to speak about demons.

So instead of using today's world terms, they were using symbolic languages such as other gods, false gods, baal, and various descriptions of powers and forces opposing God's covenant. And Israel is condemned by God for sacrificing to them.

A few times, though, there were references using such terms as "evil spirits." Nevertheless, in places where such terms were used, the reader is left with more questions. Here are a few examples:

Evil Spirit from the Lord

In Judges 9:23, the Bible says that:

> *"God sent an evil spirit between Abimelech and the lords of Shechem. So the men of Shechem dealt treacherously with Abimelech."*

Again, in 1 Samuel 16:14, the Bible says:

> *"Now, the Spirit of the LORD had departed from Saul, and an evil spirit from the LORD tormented him"* (See also 1 Samuel 18:10; 19:9).

One may ask, "You mean that God sent an evil spirit against these guys or what?"

Not exactly as it sounds. God doesn't have demons living with Him up there in heaven that he sends errands to punish some folks when they err. What happened there is that there have been some severe cases of disobedience to God's laws and instructions. Abimelech, for example, had killed 70 sons of Gideon and became a judge by *coup d'etat*. While Saul, on the other hand, had become rebellious.

When people carry out wickedness, God withdraws His protective presence and blessings; and when that happens, evil spirits – demons – gains access to foment trouble in the lives of the people involved.

In the cases mentioned, the spirit of confusion and depression worked their ways into Abimelech and Saul.

In today's life application, this can play out in a variety of ways. Here's a testimony sent in by Rebecca. She said:

"Recently, I joined a church (a national denomination) and thought I had found a home. The people were very loving and beyond welcoming. Services consisted of a lot of signs and wonders, including prophecy, but no real "preaching."

I grew up in a Pentecostal Church, so I'm used to seeing the Holy Spirit move in mighty ways as evidenced by miracles and other phenomena. Yet it seemed that every time I was in this Church or listening to their services, a spirit of confusion would come upon me. And I mean come upon me. I could not read my Bible - it seemed like the words made no sense. I could not sleep - I had awful dreams and visions. I could not eat - I had lost all appetite for food. I could not be around other people - there were anger and hatred inside of me that spilled forth every time I opened my mouth.

I literally trembled with fear constantly but had no idea what I was afraid of. At one point, I even thought of going to the local hospital because I was sure something was wrong. But I kept praying.

And for the first time in forty-three years, I know that I know that I know that the Lord spoke to me. He said to stay up under Him and draw closer to Him, and He would give me joy, unlike any I had ever seen before. For days, I was so happy. And I started reading about David and Saul. When I read about the evil spirit that God sent, I too was taken aback and began to wonder how that was possible.

Then I started watching their videos again. I immediately started to feel that confusion and fear again. I called a brother in Christ to pray with me, and as I began to tell him about the Church and how I always seemed to become afflicted with this confusion upon hearing the services, his first question to me was - they have signs and wonders but are they feeding you? And the answer is no, they aren't. I thought that the devil was attacking me because I was getting closer to Jesus. Now I know that because I was involved in something that was not from the Holy Spirit and not in line with His Word, I had placed myself outside of the presence of the Lord. And when I am outside of that presence, I am open to those attacks.

No, I don't think God put that evil spirit there specifically for me. But because I withdrew from Him, I was open for the spirit to come upon me. It is only in His presence that I am safe from confusion and fear. It is only when I am up under Him and when I draw closer to Him that I am protected, and my mind is at ease with a joy unlike any I have ever known before.

Being under Him and closer to Him means relying on His Word to lead me, not the nice people who go there. I thank God for this article. It confirms all that I have been reading in my Bible and what God has been telling me. Praise God!"

The same thing that happened to Saul and Abimelech is still happening today. When we walk out of God's will, walk out of His Word and presence and become rebellious and stubborn to the Holy Spirit, we open ourselves up to evil spirits to torment us.

God is not going to say, *"Hey, you evil spirit, go and torture that my child. Teach him a good lesson."* Not at all. It just happens that because we are out of His presence, we're exposed to attacks from the enemy.

The Prince of Persia

The book of Daniel Chapter nine and ten contains another powerful reference indicating the activities of demonic spirits. Chapter 10: 13 says,

> *But for twenty-one days the mighty Evil*
> *Spirit who overrules the kingdom of*
> *Persia blocked my way. Then Michael, one*
> *of the top officers of the heavenly army,*
> *came to help me so that I was able to*
> *break through these spirit rulers of Persia.*
> *(TLB)*

Daniel had been fasting and praying for several days. When an angel finally came to talk to him about his prayer, he first reports to him that he was delayed by a demonic spirit that engaged him in a fierce battle. He called this spirit, ***"The Prince of Persia."*** The Living Bible used such words as *"mighty Evil Spirit who overrules the kingdom of Persia."*

First, this is a fascinating illustration, indicating some organizational structure or ranking among demons. Secondly, it also gives us one of the few glimpses behind the curtains of history into engagements between demons and angels and the spiritual war that we face regarding our prayers and their answers.

This story teaches us about the reality of controlling spirits, or what you'd call territorial demons. That is, demons that control territories, environments, communities, states, or geographical locations. These demons enforce satanic agendas in the environment where they control, wage war against the Gospel, and influence specific lifestyles in such environments. Usually, evangelism and successful church planting in these environments are not possible until these territorial demons are recognized, bound in prayers and commanded to stop operations.

Goat and Calf Idols

Other Old Testament references to demons include goat idols. Leviticus 17:7 says: *"And they shall no more offer their sacrifices unto devils, after whom they have gone a whoring. This shall be a statute for ever unto them throughout their generations."*

This was talking about the golden calf idols that the Israelites had erected and worshipped in the wilderness. Here, they were called devils because idols are not just sticks and moldings. Spirits are invoked in them, and that's what the worship is all about – to the spirits behind the idols. The Amplified Bible renders that scripture this way:

So they shall no longer offer their sacrifices to goat-idols or demons or field spirits with which they have played the prostitute. This shall be a permanent statute for them throughout their generations.

The goat idol worship was a common practice in Egypt. This goat god was said to be responsible for fertility and procreation. The Egyptians worshipped it to invoke fertility on their land and people by having sex with goats brought before it for sacrifice. Somehow, it seemed that the Israelites learned this while in Egypt, and at every opportunity, they reverted to this worship, and God would punish them for that.

The point here is that when the Bible talks about idols, it is more than physical moldings and statues. It is talking about demons because the statues and moldings represent demons.

Others

Apart from the few references above, there are a couple of other places in the Old Testament that talked about the operation of demons, using such terms as:

- Deceiving spirits (1 Kings 22:19-23; 2 Chron 18:18-22).

- Spirits of distortion (Isaiah 19:14)

- Spirits of confusion

- Night creatures (Isa 34:14)

- "Spirits" or "gods" coming up from the ground (1 Sam 28:13)

The bottomline is that the Old Testament testifies to the existence of demonic beings in conflict with God and His people. These demonic spirits are found throughout the Old Testament narratives, hymns, and prophetic speeches. While they are not discussed in unambiguous terms as we see in the New Testament, we have enough hints to understand their existence and operation. These beings are associated with *idolatry and identified with heathen gods,* which implies that behind these idols (gods) was these evil forces.

Another truth to never forget from the foregoing is that demonic powers only thrive where there have been some open doors created for them, either through disobedience, rebellion or stubbornness to the instructions of God. So, in dealing with demons, we must point people to the love of God, His saving power and counsel them to surrender to a new life in Christ through the Holy Spirit. That's the perfect way to be free from demonic works and attacks.

When people carry out wickedness, God withdraws His protective presence and blessings; and when that happens, evil spirits – demons – gains access to foment trouble in the lives of the people involved.

4

HOW JESUS RESPONDED TO DEMONS

The New Testament is the fulfillment of the Old Testament. While the Old Testament was a shadow of the subjects it discussed, the New Testament is the reality of those issues.

In life, when the reality appears, the shadow disappears.

The New Testament is the reality of the shadows in the Old Testament.

Whereas the Old Testament talked about demons in ways that need teaching and interpretation to understand, the New

Testament dealt with the subject in such a way that the reader can easily see that demons are real and a significant subject.

On many occasions, Jesus confronted situations that were a result of demon possession or oppression. A decent amount of his time in ministry was spent talking about demons and resisting and driving them out. Here are ten such scenarios and how He responded.

1. His Temptation

(Matthew 4:1-11; Mark 1:12-13; Luke 4:1-13)

Jesus didn't joke with the devil. He knew that satan comes only to steal, to kill, and to destroy. He approached his handling of the devil as a life or death matter.

When satan came to tempt Him, He didn't go into a dialogue with him. He knew that human reasoning cannot send the devil away. He resisted all of the temptations by declaring scriptures, and satan departed.

Afterwards, angels came and ministered to Him.

The story of Christ's temptation and His victory is a template for us on how to handle the devil. Jesus continuously declared the WORD of God and obtained victory. That's how we are to deal with tempting situations and attacks from the enemy – We continue to declare the WORD until victory is obtained.

2. The Demon-Possessed Man

21And they went into Capernaum, and straightway on the sabbath day, he entered into the synagogue and taught.

22 And they were astonished at his doctrine: for he taught them as one that had authority, and not as the scribes.

23 And there was in their synagogue a man with an unclean spirit, and he cried out,

24 Saying, Let us alone; what have we to do with thee, thou Jesus of Nazareth? Art thou come to destroy us? I know thee who thou art, the Holy One of God.

25 And Jesus rebuked him, saying, Hold thy peace, and come out of him.

26 And when the unclean spirit had torn him and cried with a loud voice, he came out of him.

27 And they were all amazed, insomuch that they questioned among themselves, saying, What thing is this? What new doctrine is this? For with authority commandeth, he even the unclean spirits, and they do obey him.

28 And immediately his fame spread abroad throughout all the region round about Galilee. - **(Mark 1:21-28; See also Luke 4:31-37)**

While He was teaching in a synagogue in Capernaum, Jesus was confronted by a man possessed by a demon. He cried out, *"What have you to do with us, Jesus of Nazareth? Have you come to destroy us before our time? I know who you are—the Holy One of God!"*

Jesus commanded the evil spirit to be quiet and to come out of the man. The man shook, and with a loud cry, the demon left the man.

Today, there are equally many people, either possessed or oppressed, by demons in our churches. We must accept the ministry of Christ in its totality and begin to rebuke and command these demons to leave and set the captives free in the name of Jesus Christ. That's the only way we can adequately help people.

3. The Legion

(Matthew. 8:28-34, Mark 5:1-20 and Luke 8:26-39).

Jesus and His disciples were traveling in the region of the Gerasenes. When they arrived there, a man who had been living in the graveyards because of demonic possession, approached Jesus and fell flat before him, crying out, "Jesus, thou Son of the Most High God, what have you come to do with us?"

The demons begged him, "Do not torment us."

"What is your name?" Jesus asked.

They answered, "Legion, for we are many."

They begged Jesus not to drive them away from that region and requested, "If you send us out, send us into the flock of swine."

He allowed them to enter the nearby flock of swine. The pigs ran down into the sea and drowned. The man was set free and subsequently went from town to town telling everyone about the great things Jesus had done for him.

4. The Possessed Man, Blind and Dumb

22 Then was brought unto him one possessed with a devil, blind, and dumb: and he healed him, insomuch that the blind and dumb both spake and saw.

23 And all the people were amazed, and said, Is not this the son of David?

24 But when the Pharisees heard it, they said, This fellow doth not cast out devils, but by Beelzebub, the prince of the devils. - Matthew 12:22-32, Mark 3:20-30; Luke 11:14-26)

The Pharisees, the Sadducees, and the members who worshipped in the synagogue seemed to know situations caused by evil spirits, but they couldn't do anything to help because they lacked the power. They even knew demons by names. But they couldn't cast out the demons.

Theology does not cast out demons. Only faith in Christ's finished work does. Only those who believe and stand their ground in Christ can.

After Jesus cast out a demon from this man, his speech was restored, and he also began to see.

Can you imagine that?

That means that this man's suffering was a direct product of demons. It was demons that blinded him, made him dumb, and tormented him.

There are many such people in our churches today. Demons have blinded them, either spiritually or physically, and made them dumb. They can't see the power in God's word, are never growing, and are always stuck in their shells, unable to speak out and declare who they are in Christ. We sometimes see them as having personality issues, and sometimes even conclude that that's how they are. Unfortunately, their problems are demonic. They need spiritual help.

Notice that the Pharisees and teachers who couldn't help that man castigated Jesus for casting the demons out and restoring the speech and sight of the man. They accused Him of driving out demons by the power of the chief demon, beelzebub.

That's humans for you. *People will always speak ill of something they cannot do.* The world and even the traditional church system will always try to insult or speak little of those who stand with Christ in binding and casting out demons. But we must fix our eyes of Jesus, and not on their comments.

5. Jesus Rebukes Demons

Now when the sun was setting, all they that had any sick with divers diseases brought them unto him; and he laid his hands on every one of them, and healed them.

And devils also came out of many, crying out, and saying, Thou art Christ the Son of God. And he rebuking them suffered them not to speak: for they knew that he was Christ. - **Luke 4:40-41**

6. The Stubborn Demon and the Disciples

14And when they were come to the multitude, there came to him a certain man, kneeling to him, and saying,

15Lord, have mercy on my son: for he is lunatic, and sore vexed: for ofttimes, he falleth into the fire, and oft into the water.

16And I brought him to thy disciples, and they could not cure him.

17Then Jesus answered and said, O faithless and perverse generation, how long shall I be with you? how long shall I suffer you? bring him hither to me.

18And Jesus rebuked the devil; and he departed out of him: and the child was cured from that very hour.

19Then came the disciples to Jesus apart, and said, Why could not we cast him out?

20And Jesus said unto them, Because of your unbelief: for verily I say unto you, If ye have faith as a grain of mustard seed, ye shall say unto this mountain, Remove hence to yonder place, and it shall remove; and nothing shall be impossible unto you.

21 Howbeit this kind goeth not out but by prayer and fasting. - Matthew 17:14-20 (See also Mark 9:14-29; Luke 9:37-43)

Jesus was not happy that His disciples could not cast out the demon and help the poor boy. He rebuked them for their lack of faith and unbelief. Then He taught them what to do in situations where the demons become stubborn.

Jesus is not happy with us today when we don't cast out demons and help people oppressed by them. The Word of God has all the teachings and suggestions to follow and cast out demons.

7. The Greek Woman's Daughter

A Greek woman went to Jesus and requested him to cast out a demon from her daughter. Jesus replied, *"Let the children have enough first. It is not okay to take the food of the children and give it to the dogs."*

The woman responded, "Lord, You're right, but the dogs under the table get the children's leftovers."

Jesus then said, *"Wow, woman! You have great faith! It shall be done for you as you wish."*

When she returned home, the demon had left her daughter. (Matthew 15:21-28; Mark 7:24-30)

8. Mary Magdalene

Both the Gospels of Mark and Luke describe Mary Magdalene as someone out of whom Jesus cast out seven demons. -

(Mark 16:9; Luke 8:2). Then she became a great disciple of Christ.

9. The Woman With The Spirit of Infirmity

"Now He was teaching in one of the synagogues on the Sabbath. And behold, there was a woman who had a spirit of infirmity eighteen years, and was bent over and could in no way raise herself up.

But when Jesus saw her, He called her to Him and said to her, "Woman, you are loosed from your infirmity.

And He laid His hands on her, and immediately she was made straight, and glorified God." - Luke 13:10-13

10. Jesus Sends the Disciples Out with Authority Over Demons

In the Gospels of Matthew, Mark and Luke, Jesus sent His Apostles out to preach the Gospel of the kingdom. One of the instructions He gave them was to cast out demons, heal the sick and set the captives free, and He gives them the power to do so.

"Then he summoned his twelve disciples and gave them authority over unclean spirits to drive them out and to cure every disease and every illness." - (Mark 6:7; Matthew 10:1, 8; Luke 9:1)

After His Resurrection, he also told the disciples, and by extension us, to go out and evangelize. Among the signs we are to expect is the ability to cast out demons.

"These signs will accompany those who believe: in my name, they will drive out demons, they will speak new tongues..." - Mark 16:17.

So, What's the Point?

This list is not exhaustive but should serve to enlighten that Jesus saw the great torture that came from demonic activity. He did not play games with demons. Neither should we. He rebuked and cast them out, and that's what we should do.

The dynamics have not changed.

Demons are not a game. They are dangerous. But the Word of God also reveals that Jesus Christ is the LORD of all.

Greater is He that is in us than He that is in the world - 1John 4:4

Demons flee at the name of Jesus Christ.

As a child of God, you have the power to cast out demons. You can cast them out of your life, your home, from your loved ones, and your environment.

When you suspect any demonic activity, you must rise to the occasion. You have what it takes – The Name of Jesus Christ. If you don't cast them out and declare your victory in Christ, they will continue to mess things up.

Jesus saw the great torture that came from demonic activity. He did not play games with demons. Neither should we. He rebuked and cast them out, and that's what we should do.

5

WHAT IS DEMONIC POSSESSION?

Richard Gallagher, a board-certified psychiatrist and a professor of clinical psychiatry at New York Medical College, wrote an article for Washington Post, published in July 2016. In the first two paragraphs of the article, he shares the story of a woman he describes as a self-styled priestess who called herself a witch and acknowledged worshipping Satan as his queen. He writes...

"I'm a man of science and a lover of history; after studying the classics at Princeton, I trained in psychiatry at Yale

and in psychoanalysis at Columbia. That background is why a Catholic priest had asked my professional opinion, which I offered pro bono, about whether this woman had a mental disorder. This was at the height of the national panic about Satanism.

So I was inclined to skepticism. But my subject's behavior exceeded what I could explain with my training. She could tell some people their secret weaknesses, such as undue pride. She knew how individuals she'd never known had died, including my mother and her fatal case of ovarian cancer. Six people later vouched to me that, during her exorcisms, they heard her speaking multiple languages, including Latin, completely unfamiliar to her outside of her trances. This was not psychosis; it was what I can only describe as paranormal ability. I concluded that she was possessed..."

Richard Gallagher's article gathered over 2,800 comments, many of which thought he was abnormal to suggest a belief in the Christian teaching about demonic possession. Fortunately, one can only share his experience and leave everyone with the right to choose their path. And that's what Richard did.

Demons can possess someone and cause them to behave in certain ways. Arguing or disagreeing about this is not going to change this truth.

Demonic possession is the seizure of a human being by a demonic being to such a degree that the individual is controlled in whole or in part by the demon. The demon or demons takes over their mind and causes them to act and react in certain ways. Here are a few Biblical examples:

Mark 1:23-27 - Now there was a man in their synagogue with an unclean spirit. And he cried out, saying, "Let us alone! What have we to do with You, Jesus of Nazareth? Did You come to destroy us? I know who You are—the Holy One of God!"

But Jesus rebuked him, saying, "Be quiet, and come out of him!" [26] And when the unclean spirit had convulsed him and cried out with a loud voice, he came out of him.

[27] Then they were all amazed, so that they questioned among themselves, saying, "What is this? What new doctrine is this? For with authority, He commands even the unclean spirits, and they obey Him."

Mark 7:24-30 (TLB) - Then he left Galilee and went to the region of Tyre and Sidon, and tried to keep it a secret that he was there, but couldn't. For, as usual, the news of his arrival spread fast.

Right away, a woman came to him whose little girl was possessed by a demon. She had heard about Jesus, and now she came and fell at his feet, and pled with him to release her child from the demon's control. (But she was Syrophoenician—a "despised Gentile"!)

Jesus told her, "First, I should help my own family—the Jews. It isn't right to take the children's food and throw it to the dogs."

She replied, "That's true, sir, but even the puppies under the table are given some scraps from the children's plates."

"Good!" he said. "You have answered well—so well that I have healed your little girl. Go on home, for the demon has left her!"

And when she arrived home, her little girl was lying quietly in bed, and the demon was gone. (See also Matthew 8:28-32, Luke 9:37-42).

The ultimate goal of demons is to debase, defile, and ultimately destroy a human being who is made in the image of God.

The disease known as schizophrenia - a mental disorder characterized by abnormal social behavior and failure to understand what is real - can, in certain individuals, be demon possession. It also includes false beliefs, unclear or confused thinking, hearing voices that others do not hear, lack of motivation, depressive illness, or substance use disorders.

In some cases, demon-possessed individuals hear voices - voices that tell them to kill somebody, commit suicide, or undertake various kinds of harmful acts. They may have an overpowering desire to have harm done to themselves too.

Demon possessed persons may also have an uncontrollable lust for immorality. Many perverted sex practices are, in many instances, the result of demon possession.

Those who volunteer to serve Satan - the fortunetellers, spiritists, witches, warlocks, and satanists - are also possessed by demons.

In scripture, those who were possessed by demons showed certain symptoms, such as:

1. Cannot Control Themselves

A person who is under the influence of a demon cannot control themselves. The evil spirit can speak through their lips or can make them mute as it so desires. The Scripture gives examples of demon-possessed people who were dumb.

2. New Personality

Demon-possession means that a new personality is hosted in a person - the victim becomes a different person. The

Gadarene demoniac acted and spoke as one who was controlled by another character.

Suddenly they shouted, *"What have you to do with us, Son of God? Have you come here to torment us before the time?"* (Matthew 8:29).

3. Different Voice

Sometimes those who are demon-possessed speak with a different voice. On one occasion, when Jesus asked the name of the demon, the demon spoke through the man and said: "...My name is Legion; we are many" (Mark 5:9).

4. Paranormal Knowledge

In one occurrence, the demons speaking through a man immediately recognized Jesus as the Messiah (Mark 1:23-24). This understanding of Jesus' identity came from paranormal knowledge. The demons occupying their minds can give them so much information about others that one would not typically have known

5. Strange Capabilities

A demon-possessed person can sometimes display strange abilities. For example, those possessed by demons can demonstrate superhuman power. The Bible speaks of one demoniac in the following way...

He had often been restrained with shackles and chains, but the chains he wrenched apart, and the shackles he broke in pieces, and no one had the strength to subdue him. Night and day among the tombs and on the mountains he was always howling and bruising himself with stones - Mark 5:4-5.

6. Suicidal Inclinations

Demon possession can lead to oppressive suicidal thoughts. The Bible says of one demon-possessed person, "It has often cast him into the fire and into the water, to destroy him…" (Mark 9:22).

The Point

While demon possession can be manifested in many other ways not listed here, the main thing to understand is that this demonic presence controls possessed people. Though the symptoms may look like mere psychological dysfunction, in actuality, the problem is demon-possession. We need to prayerfully discern a situation to ascertain if it is demonic possession or just a health issue.

A situation which is caused by a demonic possession cannot be resolved by merely administering medical treatments. Prayer and sometimes fasting is the way to deal with such situations.

Demons can possess someone and cause them to behave in certain ways. Arguing or disagreeing about this is not going to change this reality.

6

WHAT IS DEMONIC OPPRESSION?

There is a difference between demonic possession and demonic oppression. Whereas demon possession is the process whereby an evil spirit gains access to control a person, in part or whole, demonic oppression is the unjust abuse of a person by demonic spirits.

Where there is demonic possession, there must have been some permission, knowingly or unknowingly, granted to demons to gain access to operate. But in demonic oppression, there may or may not be any permission granted. The demons just locate their targets and continue to unleash their attacks against them.

Jesus said, *"The thief comes to steal, to kill and to destroy"* (John 10:10).

The Apostle Peter also said, *"Stay alert! Watch out for your great enemy, the devil. He prowls around like a roaring lion, looking for someone to devour" (1 Peter 5:8 NLT).*

The reason the Bible instructs us to live a disciplined life and to stay alert is because the devil and his demons will try at different times to attack, try to devour, or attempt to stop us unjustly. He did it to Christ. He did it to the early Christians. He hasn't changed since then.

Here's an example of demonic oppression:

For we wanted to come to you – I, Paul, again and again [wanted to come], but Satan hindered us - 1 Thess. 2:18

We don't know precisely what happened here. But whatever it was, Paul could tell that it was not the LORD that stopped him. It was not also his choice to change plan. He says that satan stalled him and his team from proceeding with, most likely, what God wanted them to do at that time.

The Dictionary defines oppression as:

- The exercise of authority or power in a burdensome, cruel, or unjust manner.

- An act or instance of oppressing or subjecting to cruel or unjust impositions or restraints.

- The state of being oppressed.

- The feeling of being heavily burdened, mentally or physically, by troubles, adverse conditions and anxiety.

Those are precisely what demons try to carry out against us.

When things like that happen, it doesn't mean we have demons living inside us. It just means that we may be going through some demonic oppression.

It's very important to discern oppressive situations that are caused by demons and engage them in battle with the WORD of God.

Here's the thing: Demonic oppressions still aims at the ultimate purpose of the devil, which is to steal, kill and destroy. And if you don't quickly recognize them and address them adequately with the WORD, they may succeed.

Demonic oppression can be experienced in various ways, such as:

Physical ailments: such as sleeplessness, nightmares, intense anxiety, self-hurt, addictions, and physical illness.

Spiritual deadness: such as apathy and anger towards God, a sudden interest in false religious systems, etc.

Emotional turmoil: such as constant outbursts of anger, high and low emotional levels, persistent depression, unfounded fear that refuse to go, abnormal fixations, etc.

<u>Financial difficulties</u>: such as constant and unusual financial pressures. Sometimes numerous things go wrong all very quickly, and it causes great financial strain.

In my book, <u>TAKE IT BY FORCE</u>, I talked a bit more extensively on how to know if what you're going through can be classified as demonic oppression or not. I said in the book:

Demonic oppression can manifest in different forms, but there are three ways to identify them. They are:

- Dangerous fruits,

- Discernment, and

- The demonic oppression test.

What do these things mean?

Dangerous Fruits

The fruits of the Holy Spirit are love, peace, joy, hope, faithfulness, patience and self-control. If you suddenly see your life producing fruits contrary to these fruits, then you may be under demonic oppression.

Take a look at the table below:

FRUITS OF THE SPIRIT	OPPOSITE
Love	animosity, dislike, hostility, hate, hatred, ill will, indifference, neglect, apathy, coolness, disloyalty, misery, sorrow, treachery, unhappiness
Joy	depression, misery, sadness, sorrow, unhappiness, discouragement, dislike, mourning,
Peace	disagreement, discord, agitation, disharmony, distress, fighting, frustration, upset, war, worry

Forbearance	agitation, excess, impatience, indulgence, intemperance, intolerance, wildness, involvement,
Kindness	hostility, indecency, indifference, intolerance, meanness, mercilessness, selfishness, thoughtlessness, barbarousness, cruelty, harshness
Goodness	corruption, cruelty, dishonesty, dishonor, evil, immorality, meanness, handicap, hindrance, loss, indecency, wickedness
Faithfulness	disloyalty, treachery, disregard, inconstancy, dishonesty, falseness
Gentleness	hardness, imperviousness, roughness
Self-control	gratification, indulgence, self-indulgence; excessiveness, immoderacy, intemperance, intemperateness, overindulgence; unrestraint

The table gives you an idea when dangerous fruits are cropping up in your life, and you need to resist them violently.

These fruits can come from within you or from outside you. When they are coming from within you, then they are coming from you, your life is suddenly producing them.

But when they are coming from outside you, then the outside world projects those negative vibrations (fruits) against you in such a manner that you can tell that something is wrong somewhere.

From Within You

- If you suddenly see yourself developing a hatred for the things of God, suddenly have a compulsion to leave Church and abandon the faith, that's an anti-love fruit rooting in your mind.

- If you also, suddenly, notice persistent unforgiveness in your heart over an offense, such that the unforgiveness refuses to leave no matter how you try, it's the anti-love fruit as well.

- If you suddenly start getting depressed, feeling hopeless, discouraged and separated, that's the anti-joy fruit.

- If you suddenly start having severe disagreements in your home, become overly worrisome, develop the urge to fight back at any provocation, that's the anti-peace fruit budding.

- If you suddenly start losing patience with people and start getting agitated over minor issues, or notice that you suddenly start talking excessively and become intemperate, intolerant, and wild, that's the anti-forbearance fruit budding.

- If you suddenly start admiring and loving immorality, porn, and indecency, that's the anti-goodness fruit trying to grow or already growing.

- If corruption, dishonesty, and falsehood suddenly start to appeal to you, that's the anti-faithfulness fruit at work.

- If you suddenly see yourself becoming mean, and no longer feel remorse when you do wrong things, no longer show affection, empathy, and care over the hurt of others, that is a manifestation of the anti-kindness fruit. You need to uproot that.

- If you suddenly become addicted to food, alcohol, dressing, TV, and other worldly stuff, then that's the anti-temperance fruits. Note that by addiction, I mean doing something in excess, a point where it seems you can't live without those things.

From the Outside

The devil is the father of hate, war, fights, disagreements, disloyalty, corruption, worry, sorrow, depression, and all the many dangerous fruits. Sometimes he may work things out to oppose you from others, not from within you.

For example, the devil can create events where people hate you for no reason. Whatever you do, no one sees good in them. Your good works don't seem to be noticed, no matter how you try. Instead of getting a raise, you get queries.

The devil can work out severe hostility, strife, quarrels, and opposition in your home, workplace, and ministry. He may raise the spirit of falsehood and lies against you everywhere you turn to. These outside developments where the devil subverts people with wicked spirits to attack you need prayers to address.

Remember:

...We wrestle not against flesh and blood, but against principalities, against powers, against the rulers of the darkness of this world, against spiritual wickedness in high places. - Ephesians 6:12

When people and circumstances are unusually incensed against you, know that these dangerous fruits and spirits are the work of the devil and his demons. Go spiritual, and declare these fruits uprooted in the name of Jesus Christ.

Discernment

Another way to know whether a situation is a case of demonic oppression or not is by discernment. That is, an ability to sense that something is right or wrong somewhere.

If something is happening to you, in you, or in your family and, somehow, something in you is persuaded that this is not right. That this is not how things are to be, then you've just learned the truth about those situations.

You may just sense some cloud of darkness hovering, and your prayers hitting the walls. The more you pray, the more it seems things are getting messier. Such perception is spiritual and might just be the Holy Spirit telling you that this is not ordinary. You need warfare prayers to end the oppression.

The Demonic Oppression Test

Nate Thompson of Deliverance Revolution listed out what he calls Demonic Oppression Test. He suggests that when you notice any of these signs in your life, then you're under demonic oppression and need prayers for deliverance. They are:

- A compulsive desire to blaspheme God

- A revulsion against the Bible, including a desire to tear it up or destroy it

- Compulsive thoughts of suicide or murder

- A deep feeling of bitterness and hatred toward others without reason – Jews, other races, the Church, strong Christian leaders

- Any compulsive temptations that seek to force thoughts or behavior that the person honestly does not want to think or do

- Compulsive desires to tear other people down, even if it means lying to do so; vicious cutting by the tongue

- Terrifying feelings of guilt even after honest confession is made to the Lord

- Specific physical symptoms that may appear suddenly or leave quickly and for which there are no physical or physiological reason

- Symptoms such as choking sensations, pains that seem to move around and for which there is no medical cause

- The feeling of tightness about the head or eyes, dizziness, blackouts, or fainting of hostility

- Deep depression and despondency

- Sudden surges of violent rage, uncontrollable anger, or seething feeling of hatred

- Sudden panic type feeling over your salvation, even though you remember being saved and saying the salvation prayer

- Seizures of panic or other fear type seizures that would be classified as terrifying

- Dreams or nightmares that are of a horrific nature and often recurring

- Abnormal or perverted sexual desires

- Sleep or eating disorders without physical cause

- Feelings and compulsions that is unexplainable

- Bizarre, frightening thoughts that seem to come from nowhere and cannot be controlled

- Fascination with the occult

- Extreme low self-esteem

- Constant confusion in thinking

- Inability to believe (even when you want to believe)

- Horrible nightmares causing fear (often having demonic images)

- Violent thoughts (suicidal, homicidal, self-abuse)

- Tremendous hostility or fear when encountering someone involved in Deliverance work

- Irrational guilt or self-condemnation to the extreme

- The desire to do what is right but an inability to carry it out

- A strong aversion toward Scripture reading and prayer

- Sudden personality and attitude change – severe contrast, schizophrenia, bipolar disorder

- A dark countenance – steely or hollow look in eyes, contraction of the pupils sometimes facial features contort or change: often an inability to make eye contact

- Lying, exaggerating, or stealing compulsively, often wondering why

- Eating obsessions – bulimia, anorexia nervosa

- Compulsive sexual sins, especially perversions

- Irrational laughter or crying

- The compulsion to hurt self and or someone else

- Sudden speaking of a language not previously known (often an ethnic language of ancestors)

- Reaction to the name and blood of Jesus Christ (verbally or through body language)

- Extreme restlessness, especially in a spiritual environment

- Uncontrollable cutting and mocking tongue

- Vulgar language and actions

- Loss of time, from minutes to hours: ending up someplace and not knowing how they got there; regularly doing things of which there is no memory

- Extreme sleepiness around spiritual things

- Demonstration of extraordinary abilities (either ESP or telekinesis)

- Voices heard in the mind that mock, intimidate, accuse, threaten or attempt to bargain

- Supernatural experiences – hauntings, movement or disappearance of the object and other strange manifestations

- Seizures (too long and too regular)

• Pain without justifiable explanation, especially in head and stomach

• Memory Blackouts

• Physical ailments such as epileptic seizures, asthma attacks, and various pains

• Sudden temporary interference with bodily function – buzzing in ears, inability to speak or hear, severe headache, hypersensitivity in hearing or touch chills or overwhelming heat in the body, numbness in arms or legs, temporary paralysis

This seems to be a whole lot, yet it may not be exhaustive. It's enough though to help you discern a situation in your life that is a result of demonic activity and not just some health problem.

If you can relate with several of the issues raised so far in this chapter, then your situation may be a result of some severe demonic activity against your life.

Thankfully, there is hope. Be assured that there is deliverance for you no matter what the situation is. God's power is available to stop the works of the devil and his demons in your life and family.

Demonic oppression still aims at the ultimate purpose of the devil, which is to steal, to kill and to destroy. And if you don't quickly recognize them and address them adequately with the WORD, they may succeed.

7

WORKS OF DEMONS

Whether through possession or oppression, demons aim to "steal, kill and destroy." Peter further states this clear when he said, *"Be careful—watch out for attacks from Satan, your great enemy. He prowls around like a hungry, roaring lion, looking for some victim to tear apart (1 Peter 5:8 - TLB)*

Revelation 12: 12 also says, *"...woe to you people of the world, for the devil has come down to you in great anger, knowing that he has little time."*

What demons do is very clear from these scriptures and others. They are opposing God and His people on the earth. And they are doing this through possession or oppression.

However, knowing what they do is not enough. We must also understand what we can do and what we must do.

Just like Christ tormented demons and cast them out from time to time, we, as His representatives, have the same authority and power to torture and cast them out.

> **And when he came to the other side into the country of the Gergesenes, there met him two possessed with devils, coming out of the tombs, exceeding fierce, so that no man might pass by that way.**
>
> **And, behold, they cried out, saying, What have we to do with thee, Jesus, thou Son of God? art thou come hither to torment us before the time?** - Matthew 8:28-29

We are complete in Christ. He is the head of all principality and power. God has "raised us together, and made us sit together in heavenly places in Christ Jesus; that in the ages to come he might shew the exceeding riches of his grace in his kindness toward us through Christ Jesus" (Ephesians 2:6-7).

The Message Translation of Colossians 2:15 describes the current dismal and utterly powerless state of Satan and his demons after what Jesus did to them. Here's how it puts it:

"He stripped all the spiritual tyrants in the universe of their sham authority at the Cross and marched them Unclad through the streets."

Isn't that interesting?

The devil and his demons don't count. You are not to be afraid of them. Not only has Jesus given you power and authority to cast out devils, but He also made you superior to satan and his demons.

We are seated with Christ in the place of power, *"far above all principality, and power, and might, and dominion, and every name that is named, not only in this world but also in that which is to come"* (Ephesians 1:21).

The devil and his demons don't count. You are not to be afraid of them. Not only has Jesus given you power and authority to cast out devils, but He also made you superior to satan and his demons.

8

SHOULD WE ADDRESS DEMONS BY THEIR NAMES OR BY THEIR WORKS?

Many books have been written trying to give specific names of demons. That's great, but looking through the Word, you'll find that Jesus was not particularly interested in knowing demons by their names. There was only one instance where he asked the demon-possessed, "What is your name?" (Mark 5:9).

The reason Jesus never bothered going about asking demons their names or trying to figure out their names before dealing with them is that demons and their master

– the devil – are liars. When they speak, they're lying because lying is their native language (John 8:44).

So the Son of God was not going to bother himself listening to lies. He came to cast the demons out and set the captives free, and that's what He's going to do, not engaging them in fruitless discussions because they'll try to lie.

Though there are instances where a demon was called out by their names in the Bible, the majority of the time, demons are addressed by their works. For instance, if someone is sick and you feel that the sickness is a result of demonic attack, you can pray something like...

- "You spirit of cancer...
- "You spirit behind this fever...
- "You spirit of fear....

- "You spirit of back pain...
- "You spirit of addiction...
- And so on.

There are many places where Jesus prayed like that. One of such is in Luke 13:10-17. Verse 10-13 says:

> And, behold, there was a woman who had a spirit of infirmity eighteen years, and was bowed together, and could in no wise lift up herself.
>
> And when Jesus saw her, he called her to him, and said unto her, Woman, thou art loosed from thine infirmity.
>
> And he laid his hands on her: and immediately she was made straight, and glorified God.

Some more recent translations use the word **arthritis** for the problem of this woman. In verse sixteen, Jesus said that the woman was bound by satan, indicating that the woman's arthritis was a direct work of an evil spirit. Jesus rebuked the spirit behind the affliction and set her free. And she was made whole.

In ministering healing to the sick, it is sometimes, essential to first and foremost rebuke the spirit behind the sickness, then lay hands and minister healing to the patient in Jesus name. That was what Jesus did.

Luke 4:38-40 also contains Jesus' dealing with a spirit by its work.

> And he arose out of the synagogue and entered into Simon's house. And Simon's wife's mother was taken with a great fever, and they besought him for her. And he stood over her and rebuked the fever, and it left her: and immediately she arose and ministered unto them.

Jesus rebuked the fever; that is, He commanded the fever (spirit, power) to leave, and it disappeared, and the woman was healed.

In many more specific places where Jesus cast out demons, He just cast them out after He recognized them or they recognized him. He didn't waste time trying to get to know their specific names before dealing with them.

The point I'm trying to make is this: Where the name of a demon is known, call it, rebuke it and cast it out. Where it's not known (in many cases you'll not know their names, and there's no need for that), address them by their works and command them to leave. You're not going to win some award in heaven for knowing demons by their names, but by casting them out, in the name of Jesus Christ, and setting people free.

The reason Jesus never bothered going about asking demons their names or trying to figure out their names before dealing with them is that demons and their master – the devil – are liars. When they speak, they're lying because lying is their native language.

9

DEMONS EXPOSED BY THEIR OPERATIONS

As you go through the Bible, you'll come across specific mentions of demonic activities – not their specific names – but noted by their works. Let's look at some of these demons revealed in scriptures by their works.

In the Old Testament

- The spirit of jealousy – Num. 5:14, 30

- The spirit of ill will or evil wish - Judges 9:23

- A spirit of distress - 1 Samuel 16:14-23; 18:10; 19:9

- Lying/deceiving spirit- 1Kings 22:22; 2Chronicles 18:20-22

- Perverse/distortion/dizziness spirit - Isaiah 19:14

- Deep sleep - Isaiah 29:10

- Spirit of heaviness, fainting, despair - Isaiah 61:3

- Spirit of harlotry and prostitution - Hosea 4:12; 5:4

- Unclean, impurity spirit – Zech. 13:2

- Familiar spirit- Deuteronomy 18:11

- Sorrowful spirit - 1 Samuel 1:15

In the New Testament

- Deaf and dumb spirit - Mark 9:17, 25

- Spirit of infirmity or crippling spirit - Luke 13:11

- Spirit of divination - Acts 16:16

- Deceiving or deceitful spirit - 1 Timothy 4:1

- The spirit of fear/timidity - 2 Tim. 1:7

- Spirit of error/falsehood – 1John 4:6

- Unclean spirit - Matthew 10:1

- Spirit of bondage – 1 John 4:6

- Spirit of death - Hebrews 2:14-15

Identifying Demons

The easiest way to determine a demon is how it manifests – that is, by their works. A tree is known by its fruits.

Experiences will differ from person to person, and ministry to ministry, and may not be precisely any of the ones mentioned above.

For example, in our ministry to others, we've identified the operation of the spirit of miscarriage, witchcraft, addiction, depression, and others.

By listening attentively to the issue the victim is suffering from and prayerfully discerning what to do, you'll realize specific demons to address in prayers and cast them out.

Demons of Miscarriage

For you formed my inward parts; you knitted me together in my mother's womb. I praise you, for I am fearfully and wonderfully made

Wonderful are your works; my soul knows it very well. My frame was not hidden from you, when I was being made in secret, intricately woven in the depths of the earth.

Your eyes saw my unformed substance; in your book were written, every one of them, the days that were formed for me, when as yet there was none of them. - Psalm 139:13-16

Since God sees the fetus as a child, we should, too. Whether the baby was planned for or not, wanted or not, miscarriage is the death of a child—a loss.

Miscarriage is not the will of God. The Bible says, *"There will be no miscarriages nor barrenness throughout your land, and you will live out the full quota of the days of your life* (Exo. 23:26 - TLB)

There are demons responsible for miscarriage. These demons are associated with witchcraft and the marine occult kingdom.

If a woman has miscarriage after miscarriage, then apart from medical treatment, we also recommend spiritual diagnosis.

Bazuaye Francis writes: *"I married on December 4th, 1999. After two months in marriage, I observed that anytime my wife takes in and has a dream of seeing a red cloth or red palm oil, she will see her period the next day or within three days. This continued for months. She would take in, after a few weeks, she would have a similar dream and the next thing, miscarriage.*

"At a stage, I also became a partaker of that dream as well. If I have a dream and see red palm oil, she will lose the pregnancy. We continued with medication and did not take it serious, until we understood this must be an attack from the witchcraft world. No one told us that when you have same dream twice or more, then you must take it seriously. We had to embark on a three-day warfare prayer with fasting before and broke that power off our lives. Subsequently, my wife missed her period, and it stayed. I strongly believe that there are demons of miscarriage."

I do not believe that it is God who kills children in the womb. And I think you also agree too.

A woman had sought and prayed for a child for years. When she eventually got pregnant, she was very excited. Out of excitement, she went to share the good news with her friend, who was also her neighbor. Unfortunately, that night she dreamed where a bull hit her in the stomach and by morning, the pregnancy was gone. It was disheartening. Everybody in the compound sympathized with her. They comforted her and told her she still has life ahead of her.

She continued to pray until she became pregnant again, and out of excitement, she went to share with the same friend of hers. That same night, she had a similar dream she had before, and by morning, she lost the pregnancy the second time.

It was at this stage she knew that something was wrong. She went to see her pastor, and they prayed together.

While praying, the pastor had an understanding that the bull that usually hit her in the dream was a demonic spirit, a witchcraft activity. He gave her a prayer point and told her when next she takes in, she should tell nobody about it; instead, she should continue to do her prayers.

What was her prayer point?

"Lord Jesus Christ, Rock of Ages, arise and defend me."

That would be her prayer all through the period of her pregnancy.

Then it happened. She got pregnant again and decided not to tell anyone that she was pregnant this time. She decided to pray more than talk about it. One night as she was sleeping, the bull appeared in her dream again and tried to hit her as usual, but suddenly, a rock appeared and the bull hit the rock and smashed its head on the rock and died.

In the morning, as she woke up, she heard people crying in the room of her neighbor; she went to see what happened. Behold, the supposed friend was dead with bruises on her forehead.

No doubt, this friend was an in-house enemy, a secret witch who used witchcraft powers to destroy her pregnancy.

A simple spiritual rule I've learned over the years is this: ***if you have the same kind of dream more than once, then take it a bit more seriously.*** If it's something you don't understand, then pray for understanding. But by all means, do something about it.

Secondly, don't talk too much about your success story with people if it's still at the pregnancy stage (visions stage).

And thirdly, prayer is vital in taking delivery of God's vision for your life. Never stop praying until you cross the bridge. Unfortunately, some people stop praying when they set foot on the bridge.

The demons of miscarriage can attack in different ways. The story shared is just one of those ways. They can come through dreams, accident, generational covenants, past own mistakes and evil covenants, curses and spells, and so on.

However, when we call on the Lord Jesus Christ, the Rock of Ages, He heals and delivers.

Demons of Death

Another demonic spirit that we have encountered a couple of times is the demon of death. This demon can manifest in many forms. It can come in the form of suicidal thoughts, depression, deadly arrows shot in the dream, great fear, and so on. A few times, the victims would hate life and just wants to go.

If you sense the attack of the spirit of death, stand on the Word of God to resist and rebuke this demon and set the oppressed free. The Word says that *"Since we, God's children, are human beings—made of flesh and blood—he became flesh and blood too by being born in human form; for only as a human being could he die and in dying break the power of the devil who had the power of death. Only in that way could he deliver those who through fear of death have been living all their lives as slaves to constant dread"* Hebrews 2:14-15 (TLB).

Demons of Divination

These are demons that enable people to foresee and foretell the future. They enable people to see beyond the present and also see into the realm an ordinary man cannot see.

Sometimes, the demon of magic works hand in hand with the demon of divination. The demons responsible for lying wonders are also in this category.

Unfortunately, this demon has been welcomed in the Church today by so many prophets and seers. As believers, we must watch carefully not to become victims of this spirit who often masquerade itself in the guise of prophecy.

Learn to prayerfully discern prophetic words from others over your life before accepting them. Just because someone sees accurate vision about your life does not mean they are speaking from the Holy Spirit. The Bible says to test all spirits.

Here's one case to teach you that accurate prophetic word is no indication of God speaking. Sometimes it's part of a satanic strategy designed to lure one into deeper problem afterwards:

And it came to pass, as we went to prayer, a certain damsel possessed with a spirit of divination met us, which brought her masters much gain by soothsaying:

The same followed Paul and us, and cried, saying, These men are the servants of the most high God, which shew unto us the way of salvation - Acts 16:16-17

Without the Holy Spirit and an ability to see in between the lines, Paul and his colleague would have welcomed this young woman as a great prophetess. Unfortunately, she was operating with a divination spirit.

Demons of Greed and Jealousy

This demon makes people insatiable. When this demonic spirit oppresses people, it does not matter what they have, the little others have will make them have a sleepless night.

People that are possessed by this demon can go crazy due to the success of others. That was the spirit that made Cain kill his brother, Abel. That was the spirit that made Jezebel murder Naboth. It does not matter what a person has, if he or she is a victim of the spirit of greed and jealousy, they will be dying for the little things other people have.

Demons of Curses

These demons usually work with diviners, enchanters, the occult and witchcraft world. They are responsible for making evil curses and prophecies happen against people whom the curses are released against.

Mind-Control Demons

The demons of insanity can possess or oppress a person. When these demons possess someone, they lose their minds and are insane (Luke 8:27-35). When oppressed, the victims may not go mad but could lose their minds from time to time.

Others

Other demons that we encounter daily are:

- Demons of Witchcraft and Occultism

- Demons of sexual lust and immorality.

- Familiar spirits – ancestral bondages, demons that clone faces of people close to one.

- Demons of deception.

- Marine demons - Demons that live and operate from the water.

- Demons of Necromancy - Demons that give the ability to reanimate the dead and bring a message.

- Demons of rebellion and prodigality

- Demons of frustration and disappointment.

There are many of these demons. But those who are in Christ have the authority to cast them out and obtain deliverance. When you sense attacks of evil spirits over a loved one, come in the place of prayer and intercession and send them away.

Learn to prayerfully discern prophetic words from others over your life before accepting them. Just because someone sees accurate vision about you does not mean they are speaking from the Holy Spirit. The Bible says to test all spirits.

10.

CAN CHRISTIANS HAVE DEMONS?

Don't be teamed with those who do not love the Lord, for what do the people of God have in common with the people of sin? How can light live with darkness?

And what harmony can there be between Christ and the devil? How can a Christian be a partner with one who doesn't believe?

And what union can there be between God's temple and idols? For you are God's temple, the home of the living God, and God has said of you, "I will live in them and walk among them, and I will be their God and they shall be my people."

That is why the Lord has said, "Leave them; separate yourselves from them; don't touch their filthy things, and I will welcome you and be a Father to you, and you will be my sons and daughters." - 2 **Cor. 6: 14-18 (TLB)**

Demons cannot possess a Christian. That is, demons cannot live in their spirits and control them. However, a believer can be oppressed or influenced by a demon. So what's the difference?

As shared in chapters six and seven, possession means that a demon has full control over the person, in whole or in part. The demon or demons lives inside the spirits of their victims and attacks them from there. Some examples of this can be found in Matthew 17:14-18 and Luke 4:33-35; 8:27-33.

Oppression, on the other hand, means that the demons are operating from the outside against the person. They can manipulate others, events, and situations, and try to frustrate their target. And they can also manipulate the mind of the believer.

If a demon oppresses a person, it means that the demon influences the individual's mind or attitude towards negativity. Oppression can also happen in the form of attacks coming from others or coordinated demonic efforts of demons to stop the believer from having a spiritual or physical breakthrough.

There is a thin line here. If someone claims to be a Christian, as in the majority of the cases, but have not genuinely repented by conversion and renunciation of sin, demons can still possess such persons. A true Christian is one who has confessed the Lordship of Christ over his life and is striving to follow Christ daily. Not necessarily one who goes to Church, dances to music or says, "Praise God."

11

WHAT IS DELIVERANCE?

Deliverance is being rescued or set free from captivity or endangerment. In the Bible, deliverance is God rescuing His people from the oppression of the enemy or saving them from their trouble.

In the Old Testament, deliverance is concentrated primarily on God saving his people from some pain, persecution or danger. Some examples are:

- 1 Samuel 17:37 and 2Kings 20:6 – God saving His people from their adversaries

- Psalm 34:17 – God delivering from troubles.

- Psalm 7:2; 17:13; 18:16-19; 59:2 – God rescuing from the hand of the wicked.

- Daniel 3: 17-18 – God delivering from the fiery furnace

- God preserving from famine, death, and grave - Psalm 33:19, Psalm 22:19-21, Psalm 56:13, Psalm 86:13, and Hosea 13:14.

One of the most outstanding examples of deliverance in the Old Testament is the exodus from Egypt. God told Moses, *"I have come to deliver them from the Egyptians and to take them out of Egypt into a good land, a large land, a land 'flowing with milk and honey'—the land where the Canaanites, Hittites, Amorites,*

Perizzites, Hivites, and Jebusites live" (Exodus 3:8 TLB).

In the New Testament, however, deliverance has some other great applications other than its applications noted from the Old Testament. It is:

- Being saved from sin through faith in Christ. This is the most extraordinary deliverance

- Being set free from evil spirits oppression and possession (Acts 10:38).

- Healing from sicknesses and diseases

- Being saved from trials and ungodly persecution

- Being saved from danger, troubles or death.

Deliverance is usually an expression of God's love and mercy, not something we deserve. It is beyond casting out of demons.

As children of God, we may pray and seek deliverance from God regarding any unpleasing situation.

However, in this book, we'll focus on being set free from demonic oppression or possession. And on that context, deliverance is the manifestation of God's love and the compassion of Christ for the disconnection of a person from the influences, attacks, and abuse of demonic spirits. That's the same as saying that deliverance is an act of God's love made manifest through Christ's compassion and the power of the Holy Spirit towards a person who is possessed or oppressed by the devil and his demons.

Three critical elements are involved in deliverance. They are:

1. God's love

2. Christ's compassion, and

3. The power of the Holy Spirit.

Today, we can seek deliverance, release, relief, freedom and total victory through Christ and have confidence that as we pray and decree, our prayers will be answered because God's love towards us is immeasurable.

The price for our freedom has been fully paid at the Cross. No demon has the right to argue or continue operating when we pray. Jesus said, *"Listen carefully: I have given you authority [that you now possess] to tread on serpents and scorpions, and [the ability to exercise authority] over all the power of the enemy (satan), and nothing will [in any way] harm you* (Luke 10:19 AMP)

Deliverance is usually an expression of God's love and mercy, not something we deserve. As children of God, we may pray and seek deliverance from God regarding any unpleasing situation.

12

HOW TO KNOW IF SOMEONE HAS A DEMON

Please refer to chapters five and six. If you have read that, you should be able to understand the difference between demonic possession and demonic oppression.

Here's an additional summary to further help you understand situations in a person's life that can signal a demonic possession or oppression.

Compulsive sinning against one's will: Addictions, uncontrollable anger, lust, urges to murder or commit suicide. Uncontrollable behaviors like cutting, biting, stealing, etc. are almost always a sign of a demonic problem

Mental torment: Unusual Fear, depression, irrational heaviness in the soul, hearing voices in the mind, hearing loud voices that nobody else hears, obsessive thoughts, compulsive anxiety, etc. are signs of a demonic problem.

Emotional problems: Feeling rejected for no concrete reason, loneliness, constant emotional breakdowns, and regular self-isolations. However, more than just casting out demons is needed in this category; inner healing must also take place as well.

Physical health problems: If it defies medical analysis, then it's almost always a spirit that is causing it.

Strange powers or abilities: Anybody who can tell a fortune, lift an object through floating, break a solid oak board with their hand, etc. using magic or demonic powers needs deliverance.

Strange desires and feelings: such as sexual lure towards animals, strange sexual desires, unusually threatening attractions towards somebody married, or past lover, can indicate soul ties and demonic bondage.

Lineages have similar problems: If both you and one or more of your past generations have the same kind of problems, then there may be a generational spirit at work.

Obsessions: Heavy interests in the occult world, demons, and dark creatures, such as wolves, owls, etc. can indicate demonic bondage.

Obsession with death is a sure sign of demonic bondage.

Please note that every time you find somebody struggling or facing one of the issues here, you need prayerful discernment to know the best ways to help them. And sometimes, even when prayers of deliverance have been made and the demons bound and cast out, professional counseling and guidance may also be required to bring complete healing and restoration.

13

OPEN DOORS FOR DEMONS

The graven images of their gods you shall burn with fire. You shall not desire the silver or gold that is on them, nor take it for yourselves, lest you be ensnared by it, for it is an abomination to the Lord your God.

Neither shall you bring an abomination (an idol) into your house, lest you become an accursed thing like it; but you shall utterly detest and abhor it, for it is an accursed thing. – **Deut. 7:25-26 (AMP)**

God is saying here that we can come under a curse and suffer if we bring into our houses things used for idol worship. Things like books, drawings, replicas, etc.

There is a story in Joshua Chapter seven that explains this spiritual fact. The Israelites had been defeated in a battle by a tiny country called Ai. The whole army, the nation, and Joshua was put off. They went to seek the face of God. And God said,

"So get started. Purify the people. Tell them: Get ready for tomorrow by purifying yourselves. For this is what God, the God of Israel, says: There are cursed things in the camp. You won't be able to face your enemies until you have gotten rid of these cursed things. – Josh. 7:13 (TLB)

As long as they had some accursed things with them, they won't be able to face their enemies.

What were those things?

These were things dedicated to heathen gods, things used in idol worship. It was later discovered that a man among them, Achan, had stolen those stuff and buried them in his house.

Demonic doorways are things that give evil spirits access to operate in a person's life. They are legal openings of demons into a person's house, property or life. These things could be...

- Visiting witches in the past for help
- Consulting witch doctors for healing
- Using magic or reading occult books
- Seeking the help of fortune tellers, false seers, and visioners in the past
- Unholy agreements, soul ties and vows
- Using things dedicated to demons

- Generational curses (demons holding on to past parental connections)
- Witchcraft foods in the dream or physically,
- Wrong use of words,
- Laying on of hands of fake prophets,
- Sexual sins
- Addictions and drug abuse
- Lack of rest
- Fear,
- Etc.

While one may just be a victim of coordinated attacks from satan meant to hinder God's will for their life, in most cases, there's usually something the demons are holding onto.

One's actions or inactions, thoughts, words, statements or decrees can become opening for demons to come and possess or oppress a person or a home.

In seeking deliverance, always remember that not knowing that something happened does not mean it didn't happen.

For instance, you may not genuinely know that your parents took you to a river for bathing and prayer while you were a baby, but that doesn't nullify the fact that they did that. It's not your fault, yes. But it happened and has opened a door for demons to attack and carry out different forms of activities in your life and home.

Now, you have to come in the place of prayer and renounce those activities and send the demons using them as reasons packing.

That one does not know that some things happened or were used for demonic purposes and brings them into their house does not stop the fact that those things were used for demonic purposes.

If you go to the market and mistakenly buy a token that was used for witchcraft and bring it to your house, you may not know it was used for witchcraft, but your not knowing about it does not cancel the fact that it was used for witchcraft purpose.

Ignorance of action is not a cancellation of that action.

But the good news is that when we pray, the power of God will neutralize whatever is not of God and deliver victory into our hands.

Some people have asked and said, *"How can I detect the exact things that are the doorways for evil spirits into my life and home?"*

When we pray with an open mind and seek the LORD, the Holy Spirit will lead us to make the right calls and take away what belongs to the devil that is in our possession. However, even when we couldn't find any objects to remove, we must believe our prayers and not entertain fear. We must stand in our victory and keep praising God for our freedom in Christ.

One's actions or inactions, thoughts, words, statements or decrees can become opening for demons to come and possess or oppress a person or a home.

14

DO CHRISTIANS NEED DELIVERANCE?

"For we wrestle not against flesh and blood, but against principalities, against powers, against the rulers of the darkness of this world, against spiritual wickedness in high places." - Ephesians 6:12

Yes. Yes. Yes.

A Christian can need deliverance from time to time.

While demons may not possess a Christian, a Christian may be oppressed by demons.

A Christian may face coordinated attacks from demonic spirits, such that he will have many hindrances, restrictions and numerous setbacks that prevent them from receiving healing or experiencing a spiritual and physical breakthrough. This is possible because we are in ongoing warfare. The devil, the arch-enemy of God and man, is doing all he can to cause men to lose faith in God's love.

In one way, deliverance is the process of enacting our victory in Christ through spiritual warfare. We stand on the Word of God and speak to the demons and their perceived works to cease operation in Jesus name. We prayerfully locate what may have opened the door for the oppressions we are sensing and close them.

So if you're a Christian and you can relate with any of the symptoms mentioned in this book, you'll need deliverance. You do not necessarily have demons living inside you. You just need to recognize that demons are making some serious unseen warfare against your life, home or ministry.

You must rise and enforce your victory in Christ through violent authority prayers. Not some begging and complaining prayer.

Paul instructed Timothy and said: *"This charge I commit unto thee, son Timothy, according to the prophecies which went before on thee, that thou by them mightest war a good warfare"* (1 Timothy 1:18).

Okay, Timothy is not here. So the Bible is undoubtedly talking to you and me. We must learn to use the Word of God to make warfare against the projections, attacks, restrictons, and lies of the enemy.

While demons may not possess a Christian, a Christian may be oppressed by demons.

15

CAN I DELIVER MYSELF?

Anyone who desires deliverance from the activities of demons can obtain deliverance when they pray. This is because we hold the key to our lives.

So yes, you can go through a process of personal prayers and successfully deliver yourself from demonic attacks and oppression. The Bible says:

*"Shake thyself from the dust; arise, and sit down, O Jerusalem: **loose thyself from the bands of thy neck**, O captive daughter of Zion." – Isa. 52:2 (KJV).*

In many cases, one can follow a simple guideline as presented in subsequent pages in this book and get delivered from whatever oppressions and attacks they are going through. In some cases, however, one would need prayer support, especially if the person is unable to focus due to their problems.

Whatever you decide, though, the bulk of the work lies on you who needs deliverance. You must accept deliverance, yield to Christ, and declare to the devil, enough is enough.

The Bible says, *"Deliver thyself as a roe from the hand of the hunter, and as a bird from the hand of the fowler"* *(Prov. 6:5)*.

In many instances, people assume that their deliverance is in the hand of a deliverance minister. They feel that if a minister is anointed and holy, he could just wave a handkerchief or make some decrees over them and they'd be delivered. Unfortnatlely, it doesn't work like that.

The person needing deliverance is the one who determines whether they will be delivered or not. The person must repent of their sins, completely surrender to Christ, begin to live a new life, and stand ready to fight off the devil when he comes again.

In other words, a deliverance minister could pray with you, but if you go back to living in sin, or not watchful for new tricks of the devil against you, the problems may come back or even become worse. That's why I always advise: *"Don't just seek deliverance. Seek a relationship with Christ, and stay watchful after prayers."* That's the key to staying delivered.

You must accept deliverance, yield to Christ, and declare to the devil, enough is enough.

16

STEPS TO PERSONAL DELIVERANCE

The deliverance steps below are as outlined in the book, Take it By Force. These steps are guaranteed to help you obtain deliverance for yourself, your family or for a loved one.

Any Christian, who can pray "OUR LORD'S PRAYER" can cast out the devil and obtain deliverance for anyone when they pray.

It's not a big deal. The most significant part of the work has been done. We are not the ones doing the liberation. Jesus has already delivered us from the works of satan. We are only enforcing this deliverance in Christ.

Jesus said:

"...I saw Satan fall like lightning from heaven. See, I have given you authority to tread on snakes and scorpions, and over all the power of the enemy. Nothing will harm you.

"Nevertheless, do not rejoice that the spirits submit to you, but rejoice that your names are written in heaven." - Luke 10:18-20

Those who receive Christ as their LORD and Savior have their names written in the Book of Life. They can bind and cast out demons, and nothing shall by any means hurt them.

You can bind and cast out the devil from your life and family as a child of God. Yes, you can and should learn to do that. The Bible says you should.

Here are steps to obtain deliverance.

1. Get Someone to Agree With You

If you are ministering personal deliverance to yourself, you can actually pray alone. But if you are ministering to your home, office or property, you need to get someone to join you in a prayer of faith and agreement.

Usually, whether personal deliverance or family or property deliverance, two are better than one.

Jesus said in Matthew 18:19 that "If two of you shall agree on earth as touching anything that they shall ask, it shall be done for them of my Father which is in heaven."

And Ecclesiastes 4:9-12 said that *"Two are better than one, because they have a good return for their labor: If either of them falls down, one can help the other up. But pity anyone who falls and has no one to help them up.*

"Also, if two lie down together, they will keep warm. But how can one keep warm alone? Though one may be overpowered, two can defend themselves. A cord of three strands is not quickly broken."

There is power in a prayer of agreement.

However, while this is important, it is not compulsory. You are the one who needs freedom, and you can demand it in Jesus name and get it.

2. Fast and Pray

Jesus said that there are stubborn demons that will try to resist our prayers, but with fasting, we can be adequately ready to crush them (Matthew 17:21).

Fasting increases the power of prayer several times over.

When you fast, ask the Holy Spirit to open your eyes to doorways that need to be removed. Humble yourself before God and receive direction to approach the prayer sessions.

3. Locate Evil Doorways

Think deep and let the Holy Spirit guide you to doorways that allowed evil spirits to oppress you or come into your home. He will show you things and areas that you need to address.

Some doorways may be sins, while others may be unknown objects somewhere in the house or property.

As you pray and follow the leading of the Holy Spirit, He'll put it in your heart, areas that you may need to confess sins to the LORD or things to take away and destroy. Just be open to the Holy Spirit to show you what needs to be done. The Bible says:

"Many who had believed now came forward, confessing and disclosing their deeds. And a number of those who had practiced magic arts brought their books and burned them in front of everyone.

When the value of the books was calculated, it came to fifty thousand drachmas. So the word of the Lord

powerfully continued to spread and prevail." - Acts 19:18-20

4. Leverage on 'The Power of the Night.'

The night hours are victory hours.

What happens in the night times usually determines the events of the day. The Bible says in Psalm 91:5:

You will not fear the terror of night, nor the arrow that flies by day

This means that terrors are usually executed in the night times.

Why?

Because *"Everyone who does evil hates the day, and will not come into the light for fear that their deeds will be exposed* (John 3:30).

Jesus said in Matthew 13:25: *"But while men slept, his enemy came and sowed tares among the wheat, and went his way."*

Enemies utilize the night to sow tares in people's lives because they get away without notice. But when we decide to watch and pray in the night, we can destroy whatever the enemies have sown and release our blessings.

5. Pray for Many Days

There are over 100 prayer points below, targeted towards complete personal or family deliverance, all arranged under different headings. Pick one or two headings and pray the prayer points per day.

Do not be in a haste to recite the prayers and say you're done. You need to be soaked in the prayers and have an encounter with God.

Pray until you sense in your spirit that yes, the battle is over.

Deliverance is not a one prayer thing. It is a many prayers thing.

6. Believe in your prayers

God will answer your prayers. All you need to do is believe as you pray.

Most times, you may not witness some sky shakings and fallings, or any unique physical signs and manifestations. A few times, you may observe some physical vibrations, signs or demonstrations. Whatever the case, understand that you must not judge yourself and your prayers based on physical signs and experiences, but by what God has said in the scriptures. And He has said that as you pray, your prayers will be answered.

7. Yield to the LORD while praying

Don't forget that the prayers in this book are to be guidelines. While you pray, the Holy Spirit will guide your thoughts. He will add more or subtract from the prayer words. You may feel like praying some other things or for other areas not stated. Don't be overly static. Be flexible and pray as you are inspired in your heart. God is with you to guide and help you obtain a complete deliverance.

8. Recommended prayer times

While you may pray at any time, it is recommended that you select any of the time sessions below.

- 12:00am – 1:00am (Midnight Session)
- 3:00 Am – 4:00 Am (Early Morning Session)
- 6:00am – 7:00am (Morning Session)
- 12:00 – 1:00pm (Midday Session)
- 3:00pm – 4:00pm (Afternoon Session)
- 9:00pm – 10:00pm (Night Session)

You may choose any of the sessions and pray for your chosen number of days.

There are no mandates, which means you could chose afternoon session today and pray, and chose midnight session tomorrow and pray. Whatever is convenient for your schedule is welcome.

More importantly, expect the power of God to move in your life.

9. Pray With The Word

This book will help you pray with the word of God effectively. Your prayers will have more power and produce more effect when they are based on God's Word.

So, in praying the prayers in this book take time to read the scriptures that are recommended and personalize them. If after reading a verse, you feel like praying some other way before coming back to this outline, do so.

10. Pray With Authority

Please do not recite the prayer points in this book. That is, do not just read them only and say you've prayed. The prayer points are guides.

As you read out one, spend time praying it through with words the Holy Spirit puts in your mouth.

11. Maintain a Good Position

There is no specific position you must stay while praying. You can stay anyhow you want. You can pray sitting down, walking or lying down. But when you are doing serious warfare, like that of personal or family deliverance and property cleansing, standing and walking around is usually better. However, don't feel bad if you sit down and pray.

12. Be Sensitive and Pray With A Note

As you pray, you will have some revelations, either in dreams, trances, strong impressions, or insights while reading the bible. These may contain important instructions you need to carry out. When you have such insights or revelations, write them down. And quickly set about doing them.

They may come in the form of ideas, dream, or a thought on what to do about the situation. However they come, recognize what God is saying and do them. That is what gets prayers answered quickly.

13. Use The Anointing Oil

Get yourself a bottle of the Anointing oil. You are going to anoint yourself and your environment.

The Bible has a lot to say about anointing with oil. It's used to invoke healing, protection, dedication, favor and divine enablement.

Once again, as you pray, believe in your prayers. God is a prayer-answering God.

Those who receive Christ as their LORD and savior have their names written in the Book of Life. They can bind and cast out demons, and nothing shall by any means hurt them.

17

HOW DO I KNOW I'M DELIVERED?

Let's read this scripture before we continue. Mark 5:1-15:

1-2 When they arrived at the other side of the lake, a demon-possessed man ran out from a graveyard, just as Jesus was climbing from the boat.

3-4 This man lived among the gravestones and had such strength that whenever he was put into handcuffs and shackles—as he often was—he snapped the handcuffs from his wrists and smashed the shackles and walked away. No one was strong enough to control him. 5 All day long and through the night he would wander among the tombs and in the wild hills, screaming and cutting himself with sharp pieces of stone.

6When Jesus was still far out on the water, the man had seen him and had run to meet him, and fell down before him.

7-8Then Jesus spoke to the demon within the man and said, "Come out, you evil spirit."

It gave a terrible scream, shrieking, "What are you going to do to me, Jesus, Son of the Most High God? For God's sake, don't torture me!"

9"What is your name?" Jesus asked, and the demon replied, "Legion, for there are many of us here within this man."

10Then the demons begged him again and again not to send them to some distant land. 11Now as it happened, there was a massive herd of hogs rooting around on the hill above the lake. 12"Send us into those hogs," the demons begged.

13And Jesus permitted them. Then the evil spirits came out of the man and entered the hogs, and the entire herd plunged down the steep hillside into the lake and drowned.

₁₄The herdsmen fled to the nearby towns and countryside, spreading the news as they ran. Everyone rushed out to see for themselves.

₁₅And a large crowd soon gathered where Jesus was; **but as they saw the man sitting there, fully clothed and perfectly sane,** they were frightened

---

Notice in verse fifteen, the bolded part, that the delivered man became sane and normal.

The way to know that one has obtained deliverance is that the problems and attacks will cease and the person will become normal again.

However, there is a need for faith in the entire process. When demons are cast out in Jesus name, they leave. But if there was some damage already done to the person before, like the person was sick with a physical illness, loss of weight, body pains, financial setback, and so on, it takes time for the restoration process to be complete.

While the recovery process is ongoing, the person should not think that they have not been delivered. They must continue to declare the WORD in faith and work with any recommended healing plan for total restoration.

18

CAN DEMONS COME BACK AFTER THEY ARE GONE

Yes, they can. Jesus said so...

"When the unclean spirit has gone out of a person, it passes through waterless places seeking rest, but finds none.

Then it says, 'I will return to my house from which I came.' And when it comes, it finds the house empty, swept, and put in order.

Then it goes and brings with it seven other spirits more evil than itself, and they enter and dwell there, and the last state of that person is worse than the first. So also will it be with this evil generation." – Matthew 12:43-45

One can get delivered from something and the evil spirit attacks and problems come back again, and the situation becomes worse than before.

So it's possible that after praying for deliverance and you obtain deliverance from your fears, anxieties and other problems, that you find yourself later on in the same situations you were before.

But it doesn't have to be so.

One's deliverance can be permanent. It depends on the delivered, though, to make it enduring following scriptural recommendations for keeping your deliverance.

19

HOW TO MAINTAIN YOUR DELIVERANCE

In all my prayer and deliverance books, I share the following four ways to preserve your deliverance, whether from demonic possession or demonic oppression.

1. Allow No Vacuum in Your Mind

You've heard that "Nature abhors a vacuum."

That statement is more real with spiritual matters. There can be no gap in the spirit world.

If you allow a vacuum in your mind, something will fill it. If you don't fill your mind with positive things, negative things will automatically fill it.

43 "When an evil spirit leaves a person, it goes into the desert, seeking rest but finding none.

44 Then it says, 'I will return to the person I came from.' So it returns and finds its former home empty, swept, and in order.

45 Then the spirit finds seven other spirits more evil than itself, and they all enter the person and live there. And so that person is worse off than before. That will be the experience of this evil generation."
– Matthew 12:43-45

Jesus is saying here that if you leave your spirit empty, you might get attacked with worse situations.

So what must one who went through deliverance do?

"Keep this Book of the Law always on your lips; meditate on it day and night, so that you may be careful to do everything written in it. Then you will be prosperous and successful. *- Joshua 1:8."*

Work out a system to continually read the Bible and listen to it daily, hear faith-filled messages often, and from time to time, wait on the Lord in prayers.

When your mind is equipped with Godly spiritual deposits, the enemy will not have a place in your life.

2. Get Busy for God

"So you shall serve the LORD your God, and He will bless your bread and your water. And I will take sickness away from the midst of

you. No one shall suffer miscarriage or be barren in your land; I will fulfill the number of your days." - Exodus 23:25-26

Find a place in God's kingdom and do His work. Join in sharing tracts; join the prayer team; join the ushering department

Just get busy for the LORD, and no enemy will have grounds over your life. Look for a place to serve in the things of God.

3. Exercise Your Authority and Faith Whenever Necessary

You might experience challenges from time to time, challenges that can make it look like the issues you prayed about during your deliverance did not go. But you need to know this doesn't mean that God didn't answer your prayers for deliverance. These temporary situations are not proof of the failure of prayer. Quickly recognize them, and attack them with the Word of God.

The Bible says that we must have faith to please God (Hebrews 11:6). Have the confidence that your prayers were answered and follow it up with faith actions.

4. Continually Speak Faith and Positive Things About Your Life.

Proverbs 18:21 - Death and life are in the power of the tongue: and they that love it shall eat the fruit thereof.

1 Peter 3:10 - For he that will love life, and see good days, let him refrain his tongue from evil, and his lips that they speak no guile

Ephesians 4:29 - Let no corrupt communication proceed out of your mouth, but that which is good to the use of edifying, that it may minister grace unto the hearers.

20

PERSONAL PRAYERS FOR DELIVERANCE

Prayer 1

Prayer for Forgiveness

Read: Psalm 51: 1-19

Prayer

"Heavenly Father, I come before You in humility this day and surrender to Your Authority and Power. I plead that You have mercy upon my life.

I believe and confess that Jesus Christ is Your only begotten son through whom we obtain salvation, healing, deliverance and breakthrough.

LORD, please forgive me of all my sins and cleanse me with the precious blood of Jesus, in Jesus name.

O Lord, create in me a new heart, a heart that will always seek after Thee.

Let Your Spirit take over my life and direct me from today forward.

Lead me on the path of righteousness and cause me to live a holy and consecrated life, in Jesus name.

From today, Lord Jesus, I declare that I am separated from sin. I declare that Jesus is my Lord and my Savior. I declare that I am a new creature. I declare that henceforth, old things, old habits, old self, old ways of doing things, have now passed away.

I will grow daily in the knowledge and power of God from today, in Jesus Name.

O LORD, as I pray for my deliverance, I ask that You show me doors that I have opened in my life that has given demons the ground to attack and oppress me. Guide me by Your Holy Spirit that I may locate and close these doors, and empower me to walk in Your LOVE henceforth.

In Jesus Name

Father LORD, Your Word says that if I confess my sins, that You are faithful and just to forgive me. O LORD, I now confess my sins and claim your gift of forgiveness and mercy. I thank You for forgiving me of my sins and making me your child, in Jesus name.

Prayer 2

THE POWER OF THE HOLY SPIRIT

John 14:16-18

16And I will pray the Father, and He will give you another Helper, that He may abide with you forever - the Spirit of truth, whom the world cannot receive, because it neither sees Him nor knows Him; but you know Him, for He dwells with you and will be in you.

18I will not leave you orphans; I will come to you.

John 15:26

But when the Helper comes, whom I shall send to you from the Father, the Spirit of truth who proceeds from the Father, He will testify of Me.

John 16:13-14

However, when He, the Spirit of truth, has come, He will guide you into all truth; for He will not speak on His own authority, but whatever He hears He will speak; and He will tell you things to come. He will glorify Me, for He will take of what is Mine and declare it to you.

Jeremiah 33:3

Call to Me, and I will answer you, and show you great and mighty things, which you do not know.

Prayer

Dear Holy Spirit, I welcome You into my life.

I surrender my spirit, soul and body unto You this moment.

Let your presence be revealed in me.

Open my spiritual ears and give me a heart that hears and obeys You.

Cause me to walk in the path ordained to establish my destiny.

May I never miss Your leading and direction for my life from today onwards.

Help me to have fellowship with YOU daily and to recognize the tricks of the devil and resist them.

In Jesus name.

Holy Spirit, I am here to pray for personal deliverance from all forms of demonic oppressions and activities against my life. Please empower me and direct me in all the prayers to obtain my deliverance and breakthrough, in the Glorious name of Jesus Christ.

Today and every other day in this season of waiting on You LORD, I bind every spirit of distraction and weakness. I bind every spirit of forgetfulness and spiritual laxity. I cast these evil spirits into the abyss in Jesus name.

Thank You Holy Spirit,

I am confident that You will surely help me all through as I pray. As it is written, You will guide me into all truth. You will show me scriptures to equip my faith and assist me in my weakness. For this I thank You.

In Jesus Name.

Prayer 3

PLEAD THE BLOOD OF JESUS

Heavenly Father,

My LORD and my God,

Right now, I immerse my spirit, soul and body entirely in the blood of Jesus Christ.

As I plead the Blood of Jesus, let it speak for me.

Blood of Jesus Christ!

Blood of Jesus Christ!

Blood of Jesus Christ!

Blood of Jesus Christ!

Blood of Jesus Christ!

Blood of Jesus Christ!

Blood of Jesus Christ!

Speak for my deliverance, healing, protection and breakthrough henceforth, in Jesus name.

According to the book of Exodus 12:13 'the blood shall be to me for a token upon my life and family, and when the angel of death shall see the blood, he shall pass over and the plague shall not rest upon me and my house hold.'

Therefore, Blood of Jesus Christ, erect a wall of protection over my life and family henceforth, in Jesus name.

According to the book of Revelation 12:11, **I overcome the enemy by the Blood of Jesus Christ.**

Therefore, I call upon the everlasting Blood of Jesus Christ right now to enforce my deliverance from the activities Satan, in Jesus name.

According to Zechariah 9:11, **"by the blood of thy covenant I have sent forth thy prisoners out of the pit where is no water"**

For this, O LORD, I decree today that I am coming out of every pit and prison where I have been hitherto buried, in Jesus name

---

I confess that I have my freedom, deliverance, healing and breakthrough by the Blood of Jesus Christ.

Whatever has been holding me from moving forward in life and possessing my possessions, I declare them nullified in Jesus name.

Thank You Jesus.

Prayers 4

DELIVERANCE FROM NEGATIVE HABITS AND STRONGHOLDS

Romans 12:1-2

I beseech you therefore, brethren, by the mercies of God, that ye present your bodies a living sacrifice, holy, acceptable unto God, which is your reasonable service.

And be not conformed to this world: but be ye transformed by the renewing of your mind, that ye may prove what is that good, and acceptable, and perfect, will of God.

Psalm 1:1-3

Blessed is the one who does not walk in step with the wicked or stand in the way that sinners take or sit in the company of mockers,

But whose delight is in the law of the Lord, and who meditates on his law day and night.

That person is like a tree planted by streams of water, which yields its fruit in season and whose leaf does not wither— whatever they do prospers.

2 Corinthians 10: 4-5

The weapons we fight with are not the weapons of the world. On the contrary, they have divine power to demolish strongholds.

We demolish arguments and every pretension that sets itself up against the knowledge of God, and we take captive every thought to make it obedient to Christ.

Prayer

Almighty Father, I come to You this day to surrender my body to You. I hand over my thoughts to You and dedicate my mind, imagination and attitude to you, in Jesus name.

O Lord, I pray, uproot out of my life every inner argument and unbelief contesting your Word in my life, in Jesus name.

Father, arrest every negative thought in me, resisting the move of the Holy Spirit.

I command all of such thoughts to wither by fire, in Jesus name.

Every spiritual stronghold in my life working against the knowledge of God, I pull you down right now.

I command all the false gods contesting for worship in my life to die by fire, in Jesus name.

Every bad habit in my life, causing a barrier between me and the power of God, O Lord, let Your fire destroy them this moment, in Jesus name.

From today Lord Jesus, plant in me an everlasting hatred for lust, anger, bitterness, alcoholism, smoking, drinking, and over eating.

You spirits of anger, lust, dishonesty, lying, spiritual laziness, pride, exaggeration, alcoholism, smoking, gossiping, and criticizing – by the blood of Jesus Christ, I declare that I am forever free from all of you.

I command you all to leave my life now and go into the abyss in Jesus name.

O Lord my Father, whatever demonic possessions or oppressions happening in my life, resulting from my behavior, past mistakes, or addictions to negative thoughts, words and actions, Lord, please set me free, in the name of Jesus Christ.

Whatever curse and obstacle my wrong association and friendships have brought upon my life, O Lord, let them be destroyed today, in the name of Jesus Christ.

Heavenly Father, from now onwards, surround me with the right people; surround me with people who will challenge me towards a Godly and excellent life.

Henceforth, I commit myself never to walk in the counsel of the ungodly, nor stand in the way of sinners, nor dine with mockers.

Cause me by Your Spirit, Lord, to find delight in seeking You and following Godly counsel. Make me like a tree planted by the riverside that will bear fruit in all seasons, in Jesus name.

Holy Spirit, empower me to bear Your fruits every day of my life. Help me to delight in the Word of God, to walk in love, peace, joy, patience, gentleness, kindness and self-control.

In Jesus name.

Amen.

Prayer 5

Deliverance from Curses

Jeremiah 31:28-30

Just as I watched over them to uproot and tear down, and to overthrow, destroy and bring disaster, so I will watch over them to build and to plant," declares the LORD.

In those days people will no longer say, 'The parents have eaten sour grapes, and the children's teeth are set on edge.'

Instead, everyone will die for their own sin; whoever eats sour grapes--their own teeth will be set on edge.

2 Corinthians 5:17

Therefore if any man be in Christ, he is a new creature: old things are passed away; behold, all things are become new.

Galatians 3:13-14

Christ redeemed us from the curse of the law by becoming a curse for us, for it is written: "Cursed is everyone who is hung on a pole."

"He redeemed us in order that the blessing given to Abraham might come to the Gentiles through Christ Jesus, so that by faith we might receive the promise of the Spirit.

Prayer

"Heavenly Father, I bring the sins of my ancestors before you. I confess all their sins, including the killing of human beings, stealing, polygamy, worshipping of idols, selling or buying of human beings or human parts, sacrificing human beings to idols, demons and satan, eating human flesh and every evil and wicked act that they have done.

Lord, please Forgive of all our generational sins, in Jesus name.

Today, Lord, I break and nullify all curses, covenants and initiations made by my forefathers or by myself in the air, in the land, under the earth, in the waters above or underneath, in the name of Jesus Christ.

I decree Lord, because I am now in Christ Jesus, old things have passed away, all things have become new.

Every demon working against my life and family as a result of the past covenants and agreements of my forefathers, I command you all to pack and leave right now, and go back to the abyss, in Jesus name.

Every form of childhood manipulation still working against my life, family, marriage and destiny, be destroyed, in Jesus name .

Blood of Jesus Christ, flow right through to my point of origin, foundation and body system and cleanse me from all childhood defilement and evil inheritance.

I set myself free from every problem and difficulty operating in my life as a result of ignorant childhood initiation and evil practice of my parents, grandparents and guardians, in Jesus name.

Every demonic seed deposited into my life and my body from my childhood, be roasted by fire in the name of Jesus.

According to the word of God, if a man is in Christ, he is a new creature, old things are passed away, and all things have become new.

I announce this day before heaven and earth...

I am a child of God.

Jesus is in my life.

I have been removed from satanic kingdom and translated into the kingdom of light.

I am a new creature, destined to succeed in everything I do.

I cannot be stopped by anything, in Jesus name.

I command all familiar spirits perpetrating evil in my life and family, hindering the glory of God from showing forth in our efforts, be crippled and get back into the abyss in Jesus name.

Every demonic shrine, altar and temple existing in my life and family, be destroyed in the mighty name of Jesus Christ.

O Lord, my God, let every satanic covering and cloud of darkness over my life and family be destroyed this day, in Jesus name.

Every eater of flesh and drinker of bloood chasing my life and family, die by fire right now, in Jesus name.

From today, O Lord, according to Mathew 18:18, I forbid untimely death, sickness, barrenness, disappointment and failure in my life and family.

Let every closed door, opportunities and gifts in my life and family open from today, in the name Jesus Christ.

O Lord, as it is written in Colossians 1:13 - 14, I have been translated from the kingdom of darkness into the kingdom of the Son, Jesus Christ.

In him, I have redemption, through His blood, even the forgiveness of sins.

I, therefore, make the following proclamation before heaven and earth.

I belong to a new kingdom, the kingdom of light.

I am seated with Christ in the heavenly places, far above all principalities and powers.

Nothing can stop me from manifesting the glory of God; nothing will stop me from being healed and walk in divine health. In Jesus name.

Heavenly Father, I decree right now, whatever demonic instrument of accusation in my possession, knowingly or unknowingly, let them be exposed, and their powers paralyzed forever.

I now belong to a new covenant of life, peace, health and prosperity sealed with the holy and prevailing blood of Jesus Christ. In Jesus name.

Thank You Lord Jesus Christ

Amen

Prayer 6

AGAINST MONITORING SPIRITS

Prayer

Father in the Name of Jesus Christ, I thank You for giving me authority over the devil and evil spirits.

I thank You that whatever I bind here on earth is bound in heaven and whatever I loose is loosed, in Jesus name.

This day and forever, O Lord, I declare my authority over the devil, his agents and demons.

I confess that according Your Word, Lord, I have authority over demons and evil spirits. They are subject to my commands and decrees henceforth, in Jesus name.

From now onwards, I banish all evil messengers and monitoring spirits from hell assigned against my life and family.

I decree paralysis for every demon, evil messengers, wicked watchers, fowlers, spiritual hunters and every agent of darkness assigned against my life, my family, and my destiny. I command them to become permanently incapacitated from this day forward, in Jesus name.

My father and my God, it is written that they shall gather together, but their gathering is not of You. Whoever gathers *against me shall scatter and fall (Isaiah 54:17).*

I therefore command this day, let a furious east wind from heaven confuse, scatter and paralyze every evil gathering against my life and my family in the name of Jesus Christ .

O Lord my God, I decree this day, let every demonic court discussing against my life and family, raising accusations and counter accusations against me and my destiny, be destroyed by fire.

May all stubborn evil perpetrators, and chasers, after my life and family, die by fire, in the name of Jesus Christ.

Today, I curse every demonic lawyer and judge giving judgments against my life, family and destiny, in the spirit, wherever they are, I command them all to die by fire in the name of Jesus Christ.

I nullify every evil judgment and decision that has been made and is being carried out against my life and family. I command all those carrying out such judgments against me and my family to become frustrated this day, in Jesus name.

It is written that all power belongs to God, now and forever (1 Peter 5:11).

I, therefore, bring anyone, physical or spiritual, claiming power and authority over my life, I bring them to judgment with God's Word.

They have not dared me; they have dared God instead.

And as the devil was overthrown in heaven for daring God, I command them to be overthrown this day from controlling and working against my life and destiny, in Jesus name.

Evil monitoring agent assigned against my star, receive blindness.

Let the imagination of every satanic monitor fail and tumble into the abyss, in the name of Jesus Christ.

Every diviner on assignment against my life, receive madness and paralyses, in the name of Jesus Christ.

All monitoring agents across the oceans, on contract against my destiny, spirit husband and spirit wife, receive blindness and paralysis, in Jesus name.

O Lord, I will live to eat the fruit of my labor. Any man or woman, witch or wizard, who have vowed that I will not see good in life, let fire from heaven visit them and destroy their curses in Jesus name.

I command all spiritual arrows intended or released against me, my life, family and marriage to go back to the sender in, Jesus name.

Holy Ghost fire, visit and expose any evil man or woman working against my life and family this year.

Every grave dug against me and my household, O Lord, I close them in the mighty name of Jesus Christ.

Whatever belongs to my life spiritually, physically and financially, that has been damaged by the curse and works of monitoring demons and wicked individuals... be restored a hundredfold.

Yes, I decree a hundred-fold restoration of all lost opportunities and blessings for my life, family and destiny, in Jesus name.

Whatever I have eaten in the dream, causing problems in my body and destiny,

I command them to be uprooted in Jesus name.

Wherever my blessings have been buried, I command them to be uprooted and relocate me henceforth, in Jesus name."

O Lord, let me manifest the anointing of excellence; let my hand be lifted to possess my blessings in the name of Jesus.

From this day O LORD, I receive power for supernatural speed in life.

I command breakthrough to fall upon me from today, in the name of Jesus Christ.

When I lay down to sleep, I shall sleep in peace.

I shall only have dreams of the Lord and visions from heaven.

I shall no longer be oppressed in any way in my dreams, in Jesus name.

Thank you, Lord Jesus Christ, for answered prayers.

In Jesus name, I pray.

Amen

Prayer 7

MINISTER TO YOURSELF – DECLARE HEALING AND BLESSINGS

Proverbs 18:21

The tongue can bring death or life; those who love to talk will reap the consequences.'

Proverbs 13:2

From the fruit of a man's mouth, he enjoys good, but the desire of the treacherous is violence.

Matthew 12:37

For by your words, you will be acquitted, and by your words, you will be condemned.

Declare

Father, in the name of Jesus Christ, I come before You and completely surrender myself once again.

I declare that I want to obey You all the time and walk in obedience.

According to Deuteronomy 28, as I obey You, Lord, I will walk in blessings, and curses will not have a place in my life.

Holy Spirit, empower me to live and walk in obedience from this day forward.

Help me to be a doer of the Word and not a hearer only.

Let every seed of rebellion and disobedience be uprooted from my life, in Jesus name.

From this day, I decree that I have power to reverse and nullify all curses and spells that have been made against my life, because Proverbs 26:2 says that the curse without a cause shall not come.

By my surrendering to God and receiving forgiveness of sins through Christ Jesus, no curse has any more ground to work in my life.

I shall henceforth walk in divine blessings in all areas of my life, in Jesus name.

Father, in the name of Jesus, I break any curse I have imposed on myself ignorantly. Every effect of negative confessions and negative conclusions, I erase them from my life in the name of Jesus Christ.

It is written that the days of ignorance, the Lord overlooks (Acts 17:30).

The blood of Jesus has secured my deliverance.

Therefore, any evil happening in my life and family because of my negative confessions in the past, end from now onwards, in Jesus name.

I replace all self-inflicted pains and events in my life today with the peace of God that passes understanding. May the blessings of God to flow into my life, family and destiny from this day forward.

Henceforth, my going out shall be a blessing and my coming back shall be a blessing.

I shall be blessed in the city; I shall be blessed in the country.

Where men are saying there is a casting down, I shall be saying there is a lifting up, in Jesus name.

O Lord, according to your Word in Romans 8:28, everything is working out from today for my own good.

I am a blessing to my family.

I am a blessing to my country.

I am a blessing to my generation. In the name of Jesus.

King of kings and LORD of lords, I know that disobedience leads to destruction.

Lord, I come to you right now and ask for mercy.

In any way I have disobeyed Your leading and direction in the past, please forgive and have mercy on me. In Jesus name.

From today, I shall no longer labor in vain. My efforts and the work of my hands shall bear abundant fruits, in the name of Jesus Christ.

(Anoint yourself and pray).

It is written in Isaiah 10:27, that every burden shall be lifted. And every yoke shall be destroyed because of the anointing.

Therefore as I anoint myself this moment, I command all burdens in my life to be lifted.

I command all yokes to be destroyed.

By this anointing, I announce that I am healed and delivered from the bondage of curses and spells.

I am healed and restored in the name of Jesus Christ.

I declare today *I am joined to the Body and Blood of Jesus Christ.*

Whatever cannot afflict Christ has no place in my system.

It is written in Ephesians 2:6 that I am raised up with Christ and seated with Him in the heavenly places, far above all principalities and powers, above sickness and diseases.

Therefore I declare today that the life I live now is free from sorrows, sickness and disease, in the name of Jesus Christ.

'O Lord, according to Your Word, every tree you have not planted shall be rooted out and every chaff burned with fire.

I, therefore, ask that the Fire of the Holy Spirit will trace every satanic seed and plant in my life and let them be destroyed.

Uproot the seeds of laziness, disappointment, spiritual deafness, bareness, sin, confusion, frustration and setback, in the name of Jesus Christ.

Lord, it is written that as I serve You, You will take sickness and disease away from me and my family and none shall be barren.

It is also written in 3 John 1: 2 that You want us to prosper and be in good health.

And in Psalm 107: 20, that You sent Your Word, and Your Word heals us from every disease.

I, therefore, pray this moment, Lord, take away every sickness and diseases from me. Take away this sickness from..........
(CALL NAMES).

In Jesus name.

O Lord, I ask that Your Spirit will energize me from today and help me to always listen to Your voice and harken to Your instruction and commands.

Help me to always study Your Word and follow Your direction for my life.

And by this, I confess that I will live the days of my life in health, in Jesus name.

Amen

Prayers 8

FAVOR AND BREAKTHROUGH

Psalm 5:12

For You, O Lord, will bless the righteous; with favor, You will surround him as with a shield.

Psalm 30:5

For His anger is but for a moment, His favor is for life; weeping may endure for a night, but joy comes in the morning.

Psalm 89:17

For You are the glory of their strength, and in Your favor, our horn is exalted.

Psalm 102: 12-13

But You, O Lord, shall endure forever, and the remembrance of Your name to all generations. You will arise and have mercy on Zion; for the time to favor her, yes, the set time, has come.

Matthew 7:7-11

Ask, and it will be given to you; seek, and you will find; knock, and it will be opened to you.

8 For everyone who asks receives, and he who seeks finds, and to him who knocks it will be opened.

9 Or what man is there among you who, if his son asks for bread, will give him a stone?

10 Or if he asks for a fish, will he give him a serpent?

[11] If you then, being evil, know how to give good gifts to your children, how much more will your Father who is in heaven give good things to those who ask Him!

Confess And Pray

O Lord, I thank You for Your Words.

According to what I have read right now, favor is Your plan for my life. And the time for my favor and breakthrough is now.

So I decree LORD, from today, wherever I go, my voice shall be heard.

I shall no longer labor in darkness.

The light of heaven will shine on my ways.

My presence shall be desired in important places from now onwards.

I shall walk in wisdom, knowledge and the fear of God.

I shall not die before my time.

I shall live and continue to declare the goodness of the lord.

The wind of favor is blowing in every aspect of my life and family;

I shall walk in financial prosperity and favor every day.

Everyone and everything is working for my good, In Jesus name.

Amen

God

Bless

You

OTHER BOOKS BY THE SAME AUTHOR

Latest Books

31 Days in the School of Faith

31 Days With the Heroes of Faith

31 Days With the Holy Spirit

31 Days With Jesus

31 Days in the Parables

None of These Diseases

I Will Arise and Shine

Psalm 91: His Secret Place, His Shadow, and His Protection

All Books

Prayer Retreat: 21 Days Devotional With Over 500 Prayers & Declarations to Destroy Stubborn Demonic Problems.

HEALING PRAYERS & CONFESSIONS

200 Violent Prayers for Deliverance, Healing, and Financial Breakthrough.

Hearing God's Voice in Painful Moments

Healing Prayers: **Prophetic Prayers that Brings Healing**

Healing WORDS: **Daily Confessions & Declarations to Activate Your Healing.**

Prayers That Break Curses **and Spells and Release Favors and Breakthroughs.**

120 Powerful Night Prayers **That Will Change Your Life Forever.**

How to Pray for Your Children Everyday

How to Pray for Your Family

Daily Prayer Guide

Make Him Respect You: **31 Very Important Relationship Intelligence for Women to Make their Men Respect them.**

How to Cast Out Demons from Your Home, Office & Property

Praying Through the Book of Psalms

The Students' Prayer Book

How to Pray and Receive Financial Miracle

Powerful Prayers to Destroy Witchcraft Attacks.

Deliverance from Marine Spirits

Deliverance From Python Spirit

Anger Management God's Way

How God Speaks to You

Deliverance of the Mind

20 Commonly Asked Questions About Demons

Praying the Promises of God

When God Is Silent! What to Do When Prayer Seems Unanswered or Delayed

I SHALL NOT DIE: Prayers to Overcome the Spirit and Fear of Death.

Praise Warfare

Prayers to Find a Godly Spouse

How to Exercise Authority Over Sickness

Under His Shadow: Praying the Promises of God for Protection (Book 2).

Audio Books

120 Powerful Night Prayers that Will Change Your Life

28 Days of Praise Challenge: Dealing With Your Fears and Battles Through Intentional Praise

Anger Management God's Way: Bible Ways to Control Your Emotions, Get Healed of Hurts & Respond to Offenses ...Plus Powerful Daily Prayers to Overcome Bad Anger Permanently

By His Stripes: God's Promises & Prayers for Healing

Deliverance of the mind: Powerful Prayers to Deal With Mind Control, Fear, Anxiety, Depression, Anger and Other Negative Emotions.

Healing Words: Daily Confessions & Declarations to Activate Your Healing

How God Speaks to You: An ABC Guide to Hearing the Voice of God & Following His Direction for Your Life

How to Exercise Authority Over Sickness: Authoritative Prayers and Declarations for Personal Healing, and Healing of Your Loved Ones

How to Meditate on God's Word: Fast and Easy Ways to Practice Intentional Bible Meditation and Grow in Faith, Worship, and Prayer

Prayers to Find a Godly Spouse: Meditations, Prophetic Declarations and Biblical Foundation for Finding a Life Partner

Praying the Promises of God for Daily Blessings and Breakthrough

Take it By Force: 200 Violent Prayers for Deliverance, Healing and Financial Breakthrough

Under His Shadow: God's Promises and Prayers for Protection

When God Is Silent: What to Do When Prayers Seems Unanswered or Delayed

Beside the Still Waters: God's Promises and Prayers for Guidance and Direction | Learn to Know the Will of God & Make Right Decisions

Less Panic More Hope: God's Promises and Prayers to Overcome Fear, Anxiety, and Depression – Scriptures and Prayers for Mental Health

How to Pray for Your Family: Plus Over 70 Prayers for Your Family's Salvation, Healing, Restoration, and Breakthrough

Prayers that Break Curses: Everything You Need to Know About Curses, and Powerful Prayers to Stop All Kinds of Curses

20 Commonly Asked Questions About Demons: Answers You Need to Bind and Cast Out Demons, Heal the Sick, and Experience Breakthrough

Deliverance by Fire: 21 Days of Intensive Word Immersion, and Fire Prayers for Total Healing, Deliverance, Breakthrough, and Divine Intervention.

Command Your Money: Powerful Keys to Provoke Financial Breakthrough | 10 Simple Actions of Faith That Will Provoke Financial Breakthrough for Anyone in 30 Days or Less

Get in Touch

We love testimonies. We love to hear what God is doing around the world as people draw close to Him in prayer. Please share your story with us.

Also, please consider giving this book a review on Amazon and checking out our other titles at: amazon.com/author/danielokpara .

Kindly do checkout our website at www.BetterLifeWorld.org, and send us your prayer request. As we join faith with you, God's power will be made manifest in your life.

About the Author

Daniel Chika Okpara is an influential voice in contemporary Christian ministry. His mandate is to make lives better through the teaching and preaching of God's Word with signs and wonders. He is the resident pastor of Shining Light Christian Centre, a fast-growing church in the city of Lagos.

He is also the president and CEO of Better Life World Outreach Center, a non-denominational ministry dedicated to global evangelism, prayer revival, and empowering of God's people with the WORD to make their lives better. Through his Breakthrough Prayers Foundation (www.breakthroughprayers.org), an online portal leading people all over the world to encounter God and change their lives through prayer, thousands of people encounter God through prayer, and hundreds of testimonies are received from all around the world.

As a foremost Christian teacher and author, his books are in high demand in prayer groups, Bible studies, and personal devotions. He has authored over 50 life-transforming books and manuals on business, prayer, relationship and victorious living, many of which have become international best-sellers.

He is a Computer Engineer by training and holds a Master's Degree in Christian Education from Continental Christian University. He is married to Doris Okpara, his best friend, and the most significant support in his life. They are blessed with lovely children.

WEBSITE: www.betterlifeworld.org

NOTES

247